INDIAN DAYS

AT NEAH

BAY

Photographs from the
JAMES G. McCURDY COLLECTION
at the
Museum of History and Industry
operated by
Historical Society of Seattle and
King County

FOREWORD

To Second Edition of *Indian Days at Neah Bay*

Twenty years have passed since I had the pleasure of working with H. W. McCurdy in the editing and completion of his father's manuscript for *Indian Days at Neah Bay*.

James G. McCurdy loved children. Those who knew him perhaps remember him best sitting on a driftwood log surrounded by wide-eyed youngsters while he told them tales of Indians and explorers and seamen, building a cabin of twigs or drawing in the sand with a pointed stick to illustrate his stories.

It was evident that he intended this story of his boyhood among the Makah Indians for the young people who would come after him.

A whole new generation of young readers has come along since the first edition of his book was published in 1961. It is gratifying to me, as it is to H. W. McCurdy ... and as it surely would be to his father who wrote it ... that this second edition will make it available to them.

GORDON NEWELL

Olympia, Washington
May 1981

COVER PHOTO — Attlu, the well known Makah carver was presented the silver medal on his chest by the Canadian government.

PRINTED IN OFFSET BY THE PRINTERS, PAINE FIELD, WASHINGTON

DEDICATED TO

JAMES WINSLOW McCURDY
*a fourth generation native
son of Washington and
great grandson of the author.*

QUEDESSA

INDIAN DAYS
AT NEAH BAY

from an unfinished manuscript by the late

JAMES G. MCCURDY

Edited by

GORDON NEWELL

Neah Bay with visiting Canadian Indians camping above the high water mark.

Makah Craftsman Making Bows and Arrows

CARVING A MINIATURE CANOE

Makah children inspect a skin full of oil. Both whale and seal oil were part of the diet of Northwest tribes.

MAKAHS LAUNCHING CANOES

Makah fishermen casting their net from a dugout canoe. The distant shore is Vancouver Island, a part of Canada.

MAKAH MOTHER, CHILD AND PUPPY

This Makah woman had been gathering clams in the large basket supporte
by the band around her forehead.

This fresh water creek flowing into the Strait of Juan de Fuca at Neah Bay served as a primitive self-service laundry for Makah Indian women.

A broken glass photo plate shows a good catch of salmon. The women cleaned and dried the fish.

MAKAHS DIGGING CLAMS

Drying fish at Neah Bay. Thin slices of sun-cured halibut and salmon were stored for winter use. Scarecrows on the drying racks were to frighten away gulls and other birds.

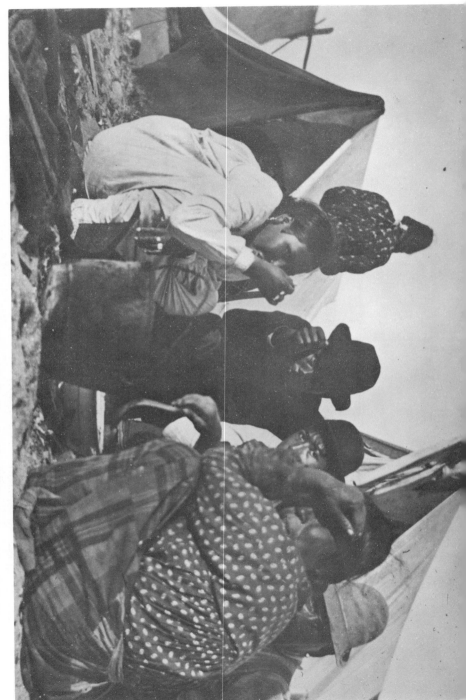

Lunchtime on the beach at Neah Bay in the 1890s.

A Makah Woman at the Turn of the Century

"Young Doctor" was no longer young when this picture was taken twenty years after Jimmy McCurdy's departure from Neah Bay, but he was still busily engaged in making beautiful dugout canoes.

Smaller Makah canoes tethered to shore as in the far distance a turn of the century steamer smudges the sky with smoke.

"Young Doctor's" assistant has inserted a carefully shaped cedar plug in the canoe drainage hole.

High prowed large seagoing canoes could carry 20 or more Indians with their camping and fishing gear.

Tlingit Indian woman in a button-decorated blanket. She was visiting the Makahs when James McCurdy took her picture.

A Makah carver and wife with artistic results of his work.

Basket weaving was a constant endeavor for the Makah women. Note the finished product at her side.

Makah woman and daughter weaving baskets from dried marsh grass.

Indian Baskets. The white settlers bought and used them by the thousands. Many are preserved in museums today.

MENDING A REED MAT ON THE BEACH

The guests gather for a Potlatch at Neah Bay, closely eyeing the gifts which are piled on the beach awaiting distribution. The buildings in the background are typical Indian homes of split cedar planks.

...terior of a typical Makah communal lodge, showing cooking places on the ...rth floor, sleeping platforms along walls, winter food supplies stored among ...e rafters and smoke holes in the roof. Balloon-like objects suspended at lower ...vel are sealskins full of oil. The crude cloth partition is a sail salvaged from ... wrecked ship.

The Makahs, unlike inland Indians, frequently grew beards. This 1890's photo, taken on the beach at Port Townsend, illustrates how the Indians had adopted canvas tents, tin cups, pottery, clothing — even baking powder — from the whites.

Burial house of an Indian chief. Such structures were built above the graves
of Makah tribal leaders.

LIGHTHOUSE JACK

INTRODUCTION

By H. W. McCurdy

Jimmy, the small white boy who had the rare experience of living with the sea-roving Makah Indians on America's last frontier, was my father, James G. McCurdy. When I was a little boy I was fascinated by his stories of those long-ago days among those strange people and I am happy that he had the foresight to record them in writing so that still another generation may learn of this vanished chapter in American history.

Jimmy's mother did not long survive the trip to Portland which ended the family's Indian days at Neah Bay. After her death Jimmy returned to Port Townsend where, after a period of bitter unhappiness in a foster home, he found a second mother in "Grandma Rainey," in whose kindly care his father placed him.

Port Townsend was an exciting place in those days, for it was the port of entry for all Puget Sound. Sailing ships and steamers stopped there for customs clearance and often anchored in Port Townsend Bay while awaiting cargoes and crews. Jimmy's adventures in pioneer Port Townsend will, perhaps, provide another book some day.

It was inevitable that, growing up among ships and sailors, Jimmy should be strongly attracted to the sea as a career, but the crippling effects of infantile paralysis made the active life of a sailor impossible for him and, at the age of fifteen, he took a job as janitor and errand boy in the First National Bank of Port Townsend. From this humble position he rose to president of the bank, finally retiring after 57 years of service.

He was also an amateur photographer and a writer of considerable talent. His photographs of the Makah Indians, made on glass plate negatives with primitive camera equipment, are the only pictorial record made of this tribe in the days when its native customs and culture still existed. Since he had lived with them and had even been made a member of their tribe, the Makahs trusted him and consented to pose for his camera. The older Indians feared and distrusted the photographer's black box and so this collection of Indian pictures is rare indeed.

His articles appeared in such leading magazines of his day as *Strand, Cosmopolitan, Youths' Companion, Overland, Pacific Monthly* and *Saturday Evening Post,* but he also found time to take part in community affairs and was an ardent church worker. He was superintendent of the Port Townsend Presbyterian Sunday School for 37 years and church treasurer for over 25 years.

But above everything else, I remember him as a gentle man who loved children and the gifts of nature. I can most easily recall him seated on a log on the beach, feeding driftwood to a small fire and surrounded by a ring of children listening raptly to his stories of the sea, the forest and the Indians. Sometimes he would build a miniature log cabin of sticks; then burn it down to illustrate some tale while the children looked on entranced.

He always retained his deep interest in the sea. After his marriage to my mother, Anna T. Laursen, who came to the West Coast of the United States from Denmark, their home was always open to the shipmasters who sailed into Port Townsend Bay from the ports of all the seven seas. Much of the furniture came from faraway places as gifts from these ship captains, and the closets were full of laces, Chinese silk and bric-a-brac from the distant places of the world.

One of my earliest recollections is that of being awakened at dawn by my father. He led me to a window of our house on the bluff above the harbor and pointed to the waters below. There was a great square-rigged ship standing in from the Strait of Juan de Fuca under full sail.

It was a simple matter of economics for the ship's master; tide and wind were favorable and the arrival under sail saved the price of a tugboat's services. But for me, and for my father too, I am sure, it provided a spectacle of pure romance and magic. One that I have never forgotten.

Apparently I inherited my grandfather's instinct for building ships, for in 1922 I entered the employ of the Puget Sound Bridge and Dredging Company, one of the Pacific Coast's leading shipbuilding and construction firms. My son, James G. McCurdy (named for the Jimmy of this story) is now president of the company. My younger son, Tom, died as a result of service connected disability as a naval officer in the Korean war. A grandson, James Winslow, also named for the Jimmy of Neah Bay days, and for Captain Winslow of the pilot schooner *Indra*, is now fast approaching the age at which his great-grandfather embarked on his youthful adventures at the wild northwest corner of America.

The original "Jimmy" McCurdy died in 1942 and I recall with pride and tenderness that all the flags in Port Townsend flew at half-mast on the day of his funeral.

Seattle, Washington
May 1961

CHAPTER ONE

Jimmy Arrives Without Traveling Impedimenta

"This new boy of yours is one of the healthiest, best-muscled youngsters I've ever helped bring to town, McCurdy." Old Doctor Willison stood before the crackling wood stove and rubbed his hands in professional satisfaction. The leaden rain of a late Northwest winter swept in off the Strait of Juan de Fuca to rattle coldly on the roof of the little clapboard house on the bluff above Port Townsend Bay.

The young father slumped tiredly in the hand-made woven chair beside the doctor. Life on this far western frontier had not been easy for his delicate wife, he reflected, and the birth of this, their third son had not been easy.

"It's good the boy has a strong frame," the father answered. "He'll need it, for I've no doubt my boys will have to work hard for a living as I've had to do."

The fire was a pleasant contrast to the March wind and rain outside and Doctor Willison was in a mood for philosophy. "A sound body is worth more than all the wealth you could give a child," he said reassuringly. "Many's the time I've seen the other side of the picture . . . babies born to wealthy parents, but short-changed at birth by nature and foredoomed to lives of ill health and misery. Johanna's come through the ordeal in fine shape, too, so you've every reason to feel mighty well pleased."

William McCurdy allowed himself a brief smile; the first since his young wife had awakened him, white-faced with pain, and told him with urgency in her voice to fetch Doctor Willison. It seemed days ago rather than brief hours.

"You're right, Doc. I'm sure happy and contented over the outcome. Who knows but you'll live to see a big construction firm established here in Port Townsend with the *McCurdy & Sons* over the door."

"What are you going to name the baby?" queried the doctor.

"I guess we'll stick to family names and call him James, after his uncle back east who sailed a ship out of Boston for a good many years."

And so it was James McCurdy at the baptism and on the courthouse records, but after that he was plain Jimmy to everyone who knew him. At first, of course, as he lay day after day playing with his own pink toes or solemnly viewing the ceiling with baby eyes, he cared not a whit for what they called him . . . or what they thought of him, as long as he received his rations regularly.

In truth, while everyone in Port Townsend, white settlers and friendly Clallam Indians alike, admitted he was a remarkably well formed and lusty infant, his own mother did not claim he was a handsome child. His eyes, his best feature, were as deep a blue as the breeze-ruffled waters of Puget Sound in summertime. His mouth was well formed, with a tendency to wreathe itself into a winning smile. But there's no denying his ears were prominent, his nose was not of the classic mould and his sandy hair showed no disposition to compromise itself into curls. It was observed by some that he resembled a tough little old Scotsman and should have been named Sandy.

As soon as practicable his mother carried him daily into the living room and deposited him in a well-padded basket suspended a few feet above the floor on two stout uprights. In this improvised cradle, built by the skilled hands of her master shipwright husband, Johanna McCurdy kept her youngest son under close supervision as she went about her daily tasks. Older brothers Frank, a lively, dependable seven-year-old, and nine-year-old Bill, also kept a watchful eye upon the new arrival during his leisure moments.

At one side of the baby's basket, arrayed along the wall, was the bulk of the family's meagre library, consisting of a miscellaneous assortment of books bound in varying colors. Young Jimmy was not merely fascinated by these books; they actually seemed to exert an influence over his actions as he surveyed them from day to day.

His mother declared that gazing at the coffin-black covers of Baxter's *Saint's Rest* filled him with a vague restlessness; that concentrating on the bright red binding of *Poe's Tales* made him wakeful and alert, while five minutes' contemplation of the drab back of McLaren's *Scottish Sermons* invariably sent him into a sound slumber, an effect its contents were likely to have upon the more mature reader.

He ran true to family tradition and the seafaring name he carried by digesting a portion of Blunt's *Coast Pilot* before he had attained the tender age of 12 months. This rather astonishing feat he accomplished by pulling the volumes from the shelf and chewing and swallowing a number of its thin, closely printed pages before being interrupted at his feast.

The big wall-clock soon interested him too, and he would lie quietly to listen for its sonorous chime. "Tick tock! Tick tock!" he would repeat with great emphasis when it struck the hour, as he pointed an eager finger at the old time piece. This word, if it can be called a word, was the first his infant lips learned to phrase.

Jimmy's mother was a sweet-faced, energetic little woman, imbued with the patience and courageous spirit of the true pioneer, for she had crossed the plains from Wisconsin to Oregon Territory with her parents in 1853, when she was but three years old.

Jimmy's father, William McCurdy, was a State of Maine man, but he had spent considerable of his young manhood in the East Boston shipyards of Donald McKay, where he had become a skilled ship-joiner . . . a specialized sort of carpenter who puts the superstructure on a vessel after the hull has been finished.

In 1857, succumbing to the promptings of an innately restless nature, he shipped for California as ship's carpenter on the little bark *Franklin Adams,* thus becoming the first of his New England family, and the last, to take leave of the country "east of Eastport, Maine" for the uncertainties of pioneer life on the far Pacific Coast.

Arriving too late for the California gold rush, McCurdy still caught the western gold fever, joining the brief stampede to the Fraser River diggings of British Columbia in 1858. He met with great hardships but scant wealth and returned to civilization wearing a dilapidated miner's outfit, a piece of mosquito-bar for a hat and a borrowed dollar in his pocket. At this point he had foresworn mining camps and resolved to stick to the trade he knew best; the trade of building things well and honestly.

But the bustle and excitement of the shipyards appealed more to him than prosaic house construction and he worked for several years in the Puget Sound shipyards of Hiram Doncaster in Washington Territory until he met and married Johanna Ebinger. Then he established a permanent home at the little seaport town of Port Townsend, devoting his skill and energy to the construction of homes and business structures.

First settled in 1851, Port Townsend, in 1867, had begun to grow from frontier village to solid waterfront town. The flimsy frame buildings which had replaced the original log cabins were, in turn, giving way to more substantial structures. Since the pioneers knew the name McCurdy to be synonymous with good workmanship and modern ideas, they gave the ex-ship joiner most of their construction business, for he could build solid houses on land as well as on the deck of a ship.

This rugged man with the skilled hands of a master builder was truly a hero to young Jimmy when he left his improvised cradle and took to navigating on his own plump legs. His father's work usually kept him away from home from dawn to dark, and the boy could hardly wait for his return. If it were cold and rainy when evening came on, Jimmy would take his place at the lamp-lit window to gaze intently up the roadway. When the weather was fine he was invariably to be found waiting at the back gate.

But no matter where he was stationed, the moment his father appeared in the distance, Jimmy was off like an Indian arrow to meet him, his flying feet hardly seeming to touch the path along which he sped, winding among the guardian maples. Then came the ritual of which neither father or son ever tired. Big William would catch tiny Jimmy in his big hands, swing him thrillingly into the air; then perch him on his shoulder to ride triumphantly back to the house.

"Jo, did you ever see a boy Jimmy's age so quick on his feet?" the father would proudly ask his smiling wife. "He's just like Doc Willison said . . . a little bundle of muscle and energy. Before long he'll be setting the pace for all the boys in the neighborhood."

And so the time passed quickly with a small boy and a young seaport flexing their muscles and growing fast together on the forest-girt shore of a broad inland sea which reflected the peaks of snowy mountains and the sails of tall ships come to build a new empire in the Far West.

Then, almost as suddenly as a lightning flash from a summer sky, came the blow that was to change the whole of Jimmy's after life.

CHAPTER TWO

The Blow Falls

Jimmy was just past three years old on that fateful morning of 1875 when he climbed painfully from his crib and half staggered into his mother's arms. "Mommy, I'se so sick," he said weakly.

His mother knew sudden fear as she felt the heat of fever through the small boy's night gown. His eyes, too, had a strange, dull look, far different from their usual bright sparkle.

"Where do you feel bad?" she asked . . . the old, old question of an anxious mother to a sick child.

"My head hurts and my feet feel sleepy-like," Jimmy wailed, unable to find reassurance in the arms that had always comforted him before.

Thoroughly alarmed, Mrs. McCurdy placed him back on the bed and sent Frank racing to find Doctor Willison.

The little doctor came without loss of time, clutching his battered black bag in one chubby fist and puffing from his fast trot up the hill from the waterfront where he had just patched up a windship sailor slashed in a dockside brawl. He took Jimmy's temperature, looked critically into his eyes and then had him take a few steps.

'I don't wish to alarm you," he told Mrs. McCurdy gravely after completing his examination, "but I'm afraid you are going to have a very sick boy. The pupils of his eyes are dilated, his temperature is high and the way he walks shows he is either dizzy or has lost partial control of his lower limbs. His symptoms point to a malady that has been appearing among children in some of the Coast towns, but which I've never encountered before. I'll give him something to reduce his fever and stop his headache; then I'll try to find out what the authorities say in the medical journals about such cases."

Jimmy was, indeed, a very sick boy, and he grew worse every day. His nervous system was seriously affected, his eyes were lusterless, his breathing labored, his body rigid. The slightest sound was torture to him. The slamming of a door or the jar of a falling object caused him to start violently and give a cry of pain.

Doctor Willison searched his medical books and journals, but they contained little information on the nature of Jimmy's illness, and that little was not reassuring. There were cautious references to an obscure disease that had been spreading through the country attacking children and an occasional adult. For want of a better name, the medical men were calling it *infant paralysis*.

The published methods of dealing with the malady were meagre and sometimes contradictory, but from the united experience of those physicians who had been brought face to face with the problem, Doctor Willison was finally able to formulate a course of treatment that seemed applicable to his little patient. At any rate, his treatment, strengthened by the mother's ceaseless care and the boy's naturally rugged constitution, seemed at last to bring about a change for the better. The fever subsided and the pain that had gripped Jimmy in its rigid vice lessened.

But one day Jimmy's mother was shocked to find that his left side from the hip down, showed a definite shrinkage. He retained feeling in his limb and a certain control, but the muscles had lost much of their original strength. Doctor Willison, who had been expecting some such after-effect, prescribed a course of massage and mild exercise.

At length the point was reached when it became necessary to find out just how badly the usefulness of the leg had been impaired. Jimmy was taken from his bed, placed upon his feet and encouraged to walk. He stepped out bravely enough, but the weakened limb refused to bear his weight and he would have fallen but for his mother's support. His father, with a heavy heart, watched his son's fruitless efforts to walk.

"You remember, Doc, what you said when the boy was born?" he asked bitterly. "Little did we think then he would ever be in this condition. Those splendid muscles you praised so highly . . . where are they now?"

"We mustn't despair too soon," the doctor replied with as much encouragement as he could muster. "Disease is no respecter of persons and it strikes without warning. On the other hand, time often works seeming mircles and I've seen many children outgrow things that seemed hopeless at first."

The father seemed to catch some faint ray of hope from the little doctor's quiet words. "Perhaps he should have a pair of crutches at first. I could make him a fine pair in no time at all."

The doctor shook his head. "Let's leave that as a last resort. If he learns to rely on crutches now he may never be able to discard them. With practice, I believe he'll recover considerable use of that weak leg."

42

Fortunately, Jimmy felt no pain now in the disease-stricken leg, but its retarded development, which extended to the hip, threw him off balance. When, after weeks of determined effort, he did at last walk bravely without support it was with a decided limp.

To make matters worse, his ankle had also lost much of its strength, allowing his foot to turn over on its side when he walked. His father at once had a shoe fitted with an iron brace which it was hoped would correct this trouble, but it only added to poor Jimmy's troubles.

Although fitted with an adjustable padded disk designed in theory to hold the ankle in place, the cruel brace was an instrument of torture. When Jimmy tried to walk with it, it caused more pain than he could bear. To correct this situation the brace had to be widened to allow more play when in motion. This made it more comfortable, but helped to defeat its purpose and in the end the cumbersome appliance was discarded.

The realization that he was physically handicapped and could not readily follow his companions in their more active games came to Jimmy only by degrees. One of the first intimations he had of this bitter fact came when he was about five years old. A craze for stilt walking had developed among the youngsters of Port Townsend and Jimmy was determined to learn the thrilling art. He found to his great surprise that the feat was much harder for him to master than for the other boys. This difficulty in keeping his balance confronted him in nearly every sport in which he sought to engage.

At some previous time, unknown even to himself, he had learned to run in his own peculiar fashion. It was more like a lope, with his sound leg required to do more than its just share of the work, but he could get over the ground at quite a rapid if ungraceful pace.

Experience taught him that by continued effort he could accomplish many things that had at first seemed far beyond his reach; not with the ease and skill of his companions, of course, but sufficiently well that he could take part in most of their games and amusements. Thus he came to develop the habit of persistence which was to help him overcome many physical obstacles.

But Jimmy's long illness and longer fight for recovery had left him with a disposition that was difficult to analyze. He was high-strung and extremely sensitive and shrunk from being teased or ridiculed. Up to a certain point he would maintain a profound silence and keep his feelings deeply hidden, but if he were pushed too far he was apt to fly into a perfect passion and lose all restraint.

Although naturally timid he would, at such times, become a paragon of bravery, utterly indifferent to reason or threat of

43

punishment. These infrequent displays of temper usually left him breathless and on the verge of hysteria.

His mother admitted he was "a difficult child to handle," but realizing the terrific nervous shock he had sustained, she made every effort to keep him in a tranquil frame of mind. His brother Frank had also learned not to cross him unduly and invariably treated him with studied consideration.

As Jimmy grew older, the realization of his physical handicap was borne in upon him in a multitude of ways, but in general he maintained a cheerful outlook on life and was by no means an unhappy child. His love of nature and the joy of living animated his daily existence and the Port Townsend of territorial days was a wonderful and exciting place of lonely beaches, tall trees and taller mountains, great ships and Indians and sailor men.

When all else failed, Jimmy was comforted by the unfathomable current of affection which existed between him and his mother. She was the court of last resort in all his boyish troubles and he clung to her with all the intensity of his sensitive nature.

Jimmy had entered school and had just graduated from the ABC class when there occurred another of those sudden happenings that seemed destined to mark the pathway of his boyhood.

If the raw new seaport town of his birth had seemed a place of color and strange adventure, his new home was to be the sort of place boys of all ages have always dreamed about.

CHAPTER THREE

Farthest West

Few men in the Puget Sound region had a greater reputation as a builder than Jimmy's father, so it was not surprising that when, in 1877, government authorities were searching for a competent man to construct a lifesaving station at Neah Bay, chief village of the Makah Indian Reservation, their choice should fall upon him. Located just inside grim Cape Flattery, most northwesterly point of the continental United States, the new station was vital to the growing sea commerce of the new frontier.

This assignment was fulfilled in such a satisfactory manner that the job was made a permanent one for William McCurdy. The United States Department of Indian Affairs appointed him superintendent of construction at the reservation. His duties included maintenance and construction of buildings as well as the teaching of carpentry and building to the Indian boys. Jimmy's mother was to receive additional compensation for giving the native girls instruction in sewing and civilized home making.

Another of the periodic economic depressions of that era was afflicting the construction business at Port Townsend and Jimmy's father had been considering a return to shipbuilding, though without enthusiasm, for it would entail long absences from his family.

Taking everything into consideration, it was deemed wise to accept the appointment, even though the step meant the severing of many pleasant associations and the removal of the little family even further from the last outposts of civilization. And so the family home was sold, the household goods were packed and passage was engaged on the steamboat *J. B. Libby* which made the weekly voyage from Port Townsend to Neah Bay, ninety miles to the westward.

The primitive Indian fishing village of Neah Bay boasted no such modern facilities as docks or wharves in those days and landings could be made only by rowboat or canoe. A heavy swell from the open Pacific was running when the little steamer rolled and puffed her way into the bay; along the beach the white crests of breakers could be seen and their sullen roar plainly heard.

But the steamboat captain, impatient of delay, was determined that the landing should be made at once and the ship's boat was put over the side. In this cranky craft the entire family embarked, with the captain in the sternsheets and two deckhands at the oars. A number of Indians in their graceful, seagoing canoes had offered to take the party ashore for a modest fee, but their services had been haughtily refused by the captain, who was not averse to displaying his skill at handling a small boat in a lumpy sea.

As the laboring boat neared the shore, the hissing gray waves increased in size. Jimmy sat facing the stern and watched with fascinated eyes the inward march of the menacing, foam-topped rollers. Suddenly he gave a shrill cry, for behind them a wave of prodigious size was taking form and rushing down upon them with the speed of a race horse.

The oarsmen, warned by his shout, saw their peril and tried frantically to outrun the giant wave, but in vain. As they were about to beach the boat a solid wall of water crashed over the craft, turning it end over end and hurling its occupants into the bitterly cold sea.

The three boys were seized by their father and dragged out of the undertow by the hair. Their mother was pulled from the water half strangled, and assisted ashore by some of the men. After much confusion the group stood huddled together upon the wind-whipped beach, soaked to the skin and chilled to the bone, but happily suffering only minor bruises.

The Indian Agent's wife, who had watched the near tragedy from the high bluff above the waterfront, had the family immediately brought up to her home. Here the boys and their mother were given dry clothing and thoroughly warmed in front of the huge fireplace. The father, heedless of soaked clothing, gulped a steaming cup of coffee, then returned to the beach to oversee the landing of the household goods being brought ashore by amphibious Makah Indians in several large canoes lashed together.

It was a depressing beginning for a new life in a wild corner of the nation, but the sunlight of a new day revived the spirits of Jimmy and his brothers, who lost no time in exploring this strange new home. They found the village of Neah Bay to be divided into two distinct sections. The Indian Agent, clerk and teaching staff had quarters at Bahada, at the eastern extremity of the bay. Some of the agency buildings were on a level tract of considerable size; others stood upon a grassy plateau which terminated in a rocky ledge running out into the deep waters of Juan de Fuca Strait. About half a mile beyond the tip of this ledge lay a small islet known as Waahdah Island.

A crescent-shaped beach of pure white sand connected Bahada Point with the main village, two miles to the westward, where the natives and most of the government workers lived. Some distance beyond the village the bay terminated in a frowning headland, Koitlah Point. The roadstead was open to the profound swells of the Pacific Ocean, which was only seven miles to the west, and did not offer a secure anchorage in rough weather.

Jimmy and his brothers found much to interest them, for it seemed they had been transported into a strange new world. The rocky ledge which jutted from the mainland to the deep salt water of the Strait was an especially wonderful place, for here it seemed they could leave the responsibilities of mundane land behind them and enter a solitary realm of wind and sea and solitude.

They discovered rocky aquariums created by the receding tide, filled with crystal clear, bitterly pure salt water. Looking down into these miniature sea chasms, the boys could discern many varieties of small fish, dull red crabs, delicate mosses and marine plants growing in profusion, free from the attack of larger, more deadly sea creatures.

The further out the boys ventured on the magic ledge, the better the chance of finding something new and wonderful, but here the abrupt slopes became festooned with a luxuriant growth of seaweed, slippery and treacherous as a coating of ice. Beneath, a treacherous current raced toward the sea, gurgling and fretting ominously as it went.

The boys would peer rather fearfully into the dark, troubled depths, sensing the strange mystery of the sea. They could readily imagine that in the dark crannies of the rock, securely hidden from human sight, huge tentacled devil fish and other sea monstrosities lay waiting for their prey.

But with each repeated visit Jimmy and Frank became more venturesome. Although neither could swim, they imagined their bare feet would hold them firmly wherever they chose to step. The last vestiges of caution left them when, one sparkling morning, they discovered that an extremely low tide had exposed portions of the ledge they had never seen before. By slow degrees they progressed to the very tip of the rocky rampart and climbed down its steep seaward face to secure such precious objects as were revealed to their gaze.

An old Makah, trolling for salmon off the point, stopped for a moment with uplifted paddle as the current swept his dugout canoe past the boy's rocky perch. *"Klosh nanick mikah!"* he shouted in the Chinook jargon,[1] *"Yaka hyas cultus illihee!"* (Be careful, you! That's a very bad place!)

---

[1]The Chinook jargon was a trade language composed of a few hundred Northwest Indian, English and French words and generally understood by white settlers and Indians alike during pioneer days in the Pacific Northwest.

The boys understood the words, but, boylike, they gave little heed to the kindly warning of the old fisherman.

At the very water's edge, Frank had spied a curious shell. Descending step by step, he reached down to grasp it when, without warning, his wet feet slipped on the blanket of treacherous seaweed. The sea had tempted him with its pretty bauble and in a split second he was struggling for his life in its swirling currents.

Coming to the surface, gasping and half blinded by the sting of salt water, the boy realized he was in great peril of being swept out to sea by the racing current. His desperately searching fingers grasped the streamers of seaweed trailing away from the rocks. This enabled him to keep his head above water and to draw himself close to the ledge, but he could not climb its slippery wall.

There he hung, rising and falling with the ocean swell, with the tide threatening to tear loose his grip on the marine growth which, having caused his mishap, now acted as a tenuous hold on life. Should this aid fail him he would be carried away to almost certain death.

Jimmy, although terror stricken, did not lose his presence of mind.

"Hold on tight, Frank. I'll help you," he kept repeating as he stretched out across the ledge, waiting for a chance to give his brother a helping hand.

As Frank rose on an unusually high swell, Jimmy reached down and, grasping him by the hair, pulled upward with all his strength. This support, slight as it was, enabled Frank to release one hand and reach up far enough to fix his fingers in a crevice of the rock.

He held desperately to this position until the next swell lifted him; then secured a firm grip on the rock with his other hand. Jimmy then transferred his bulldog grip to the collar of his brother's shirt and continued to pull with all his might.

By this means Frank succeeded in crawling inch by inch to the top of the ledge, where he lay dripping and shivering until he regained a portion of his strength. The boys then hid themselves behind a convenient sand dune, where Frank removed his soaked clothing and hung it over a log to dry. The contact of hot sunshine and hot sand on his naked body drew out the deadly chill and made the recent brush with death seem far away and unreal.

"That was plucky of you, Jimmy, to keep hold of me the way you did. I might have pulled you in, too," Frank said thoughtfully.

Jimmy felt a warm glow of pride deep inside; warmer and brighter than the summer sun. "Shucks," he said, digging his bare feet in the sand, "you'd've done the same for me. Anyway, I could have let go if I found I was slipping in."

Frank flipped a barnacle-covered rock and the boys listened for the liquid *plunk* as it struck the water. "Nope, you'd never have let go, no matter what," he said. "Do you know," he admitted, shuddering a little at the memory, "when I was trying to crawl up the side of the ledge a piece of cold, clammy seaweed got wrapped around my ankle and I thought sure it was the arm of a big devil fish pulling me down to its cave. I was sure glad when I got it kicked loose."

Whether to mention their experience to their parents or not was a question the boys debated at some length. They tried to convince themselves it would be better to maintain a discreet silence, thus saving their mother from a shock and themselves from an abridgement of their liberty.

They were not called upon to make this momentous decision, however, for one of the women teachers had happened to witness the ending of the mishap and, greatly excited, had run to their mother with the story. There remained little for them to do upon their arrival home but fill in the details and await judgement.

The curtailment of their freedom which they had feared became an actuality, for they were strictly forbidden to visit the treacherous ledge in the future.

But as summer was almost over and school about to begin, this restriction was not as severe a blow as it might have been. Besides, how many other boys in America were free to explore a genuine Indian village inhabited by sea-going warriors who built great canoes with the sweet lines of Viking ships and took them out below the world's curve to stalk the great whale, *Kwaddis*, on the gray reaches of the North Pacific?

Even a restricted life was an exciting one for wide-eyed white boys on that far Western frontier of eighty years ago.

CHAPTER FOUR

The Strange Inhabitants of Neah Bay

There were about seven hundred Makahs living upon the Neah Bay reservation in 1877, and many of the older natives had departed only slightly from their age-old tribal habits and customs. In this remote region the white man had not yet debauched the Indian and stripped him of his pride and dignity.

The Makahs had a tribal language of their own, full of clicks and gutterals, but when communicating with the whites they used the Chinook jargon, a primitive trade language which had been implemented by the early fur traders and Hudson's Bay men.

In stature the Makahs were rather short and squat, with broad shoulders made powerful by ages of pitting strength of paddle-arm against the power of the sea. Their color was a light reddish-bronze, except where the mixture of a northern strain showed itself in a darker hue.

Most of the women wore the universal blanket, fastened with a large safety pin at the throat. These concessions to the white man's trading post were supplemented by the traditional short skirt of shredded cedar bark with a coarse fringe spun along the hem. The men wore loin cloths with a blanket thrown over their shoulders. During cold or rainy weather coats of animal skins were added. Conical hats resembling Chinese headgear were woven by the women and worn by both sexes during the winter.

The majority of the Indians lived in large communal lodges from sixty to eighty feet square and each capable of accommodating a number of families. These primitive apartment houses were built of rough cedar boards split from logs with the aid of primitive tools.

Each family had its own cooking fire burning upon the earth-packed floor, the smoke escaping as best it could through holes in the flat roof. On rafters overhead, strips of seal meat and fish were spread out to be preserved by the smoke as it mounted skyward. Wooden platforms, raised about two feet above the ground, extended around the inside walls for lounging and sleeping purposes.

Jimmy and his brothers found these dark, smoky, pungent-smelling lodges exciting places to visit, for their father explained that they were exactly the same as the dwellings of the Northwest Indians long before the first white men sailed the Pacific. Already a few of the more progressive Indians had built small individual dwellings patterned after the homes of the white people, but even these more conventional houses had a strangely piratical air about them. Fittings and furniture from wrecked ships were widely used by the sea-roving Makahs, who considered the spoils of the sea theirs by inherent right.

The food of the Indians consisted of various kinds of fish, berries, seal meat, whale meat and shell fish. They had also acquired a hearty appetite for white man's food, however, and those who could afford such luxuries added to their larders such trading post supplies as flour, tea, sugar, coffee, molasses, rice and the more common vegetables. Salmon and halibut were their staple foods, the surplus catch being split into thin flakes and dried for winter use.

For generations the Makahs had been under the domination of their medicine men, who preyed upon their peoples' superstition and ignorance. But after mingling with the whites, whose medicine was stronger than that of their tribal doctors, many had begun to throw off the yoke of the painted imposters who had so long held them in spiritual and physical bondage. Still, the old medicine men clung stubbornly to their limited following and practiced their version of the healing arts wherever they could gain an entrance. Aside from the use of a few simple herbs they knew nothing of medical science; of anatomy they knew even less.

They proceeded on the primitive belief that all disease was caused by the action of evil spirits, which they endeavored to expel through heroic measures, heroism being required in abundance of their unfortunate "patients." It was their common procedure to make an incision at the focal point of pain and vigorously suck the blood from the wound. The particular evil spirit causing the trouble was supposed to be withdrawn along with the flow of blood.

Sometimes the medicine men varied this treatment by applying fire to the affected parts, but when all other measures failed they fell back upon their incantations and an ear-splitting din of tomtoms and rattles. Needless to say, the mortality rate among their patients was very high.

The burial customs of the Makah had changed considerably through the passing ages. For centuries they had placed their dead upon platforms resting on the lower limbs of trees. Later they took to depositing bodies in large canoes, with smaller overturned canoes serving as coffin lids. At the time of Jimmy's

51

residence among them they had adopted the custom of the whites, burying their dead in the earth. However, they retained a part of their original tribal burial rites, depositing many of the belongings of the deceased in the grave to serve him in his future life. All such articles were first thoroughly demolished so that the cupidity of potential grave robbers would not be aroused.

During these ceremonies Jimmy and his brothers watched from a safe distance as wailing squaws broke up crockery, clocks and other household furniture. Even a sewing machine, no doubt entitled by reason of age and decrepitude to a permanent resting place beside its late owner, was demolished and and thrown into the grave during one Indian funeral which Jimmy watched. Following the graveside services, the officiating squaws would become hired mourners and for weeks on end would make the nights hideous with their howling and wailing from back on the lonely hills above the bay.

The prosperity of the hired funeral mourners was lessened somewhat by the presence on the reservation of the government surgeon, Doctor Howell, who treated the white population and such of the natives as might prefer his services to those of the medicine men. Since his office adjoined the government school, Jimmy and his companions had ample opportunity to view at first hand the good doctor's professional technique.

Even this product of Eastern medical schools, it seemed, was forced to compromise with the tribal doctrine of his primitive colleagues, the medicine men. Doctor Howell might prescribe suitable drugs or perform required surgery, but first he must perform the curious bloodletting operation known as cupping, a process which his Makah patients considered both fascinating and essential. No matter what their ailments, they insisted that a "cupping" would not prove amiss.

Present day doctors frequently cater to this kind of self-diagnosis by their patients with sugar pills. Doctor Howell used a small metal cup fitted with a spring-operated lancet. A scrap of paper was burned in the cup to form a vacuum, after which it was clamped to the body of the patient, usually upon the back. When the spring was released, the lancet tip penetrated the flesh to some depth and the vacuum drew out the blood. When the cup was removed the patient would view with great satisfaction the dark blood that had been extracted from his body and grunt, "Hyas skookum medicine!" (Very strong medicine.)

One of Jimmy's Makah playmates, a small boy named Howitch, was kicked by a vicious horse and suffered a broken arm. Fortunately, his parents were among the more enlightened Indians and Doctor Howell was called to set and splint the injury. But late that night one of the old medicine men stole into the boy's room, tore the bandages loose, bit into the fracture and sucked out a quantity of blood.

Next morning, when Doctor Howell called and viewed the professional efforts of the medicine man, he was simply furious, but he swallowed his rage as best he could. Redressing the boy's mangled arm, he cautioned the mother under no circumstances to allow little Howitch to be disturbed.

About midnight the old medicine man again crept into the lodge and approached the injured boy. This time his head was incased in a hideous wooden mask and he carried a huge rattle in one filthy hand. The mother implored him not to molest the patient, but he paid no attention to her plea. Howitch's father was too deeply imbued with the Indian's age-old, superstitious dread of the witch doctor to actively oppose him.

The medicine man approached the boy's bed and seized the splinted and bandaged arm. In spite of Howitch's agonized screams, he again tore away the bandages and sucked the wound. His next step was to produce such a horrible racket with his rattle that any self-respecting evil spirit would certainly have beat an immediate and hasty retreat. Then, leaving the boy exhausted and moaning in pain and fright, the medicine man left, evidently well pleased with his night's work.

When Doctor Howell made his next visit to find his small patient in a violent fever and in danger of losing his arm, he said not a word. Tight-lipped, he repaired the mischief as best he could and then hunted up his old navy pistol and put it in shape for instant use.

Seeking out the medicine man, he collared him securely and grimly threatened to shoot him on sight the next time he appeared within a mile of little Howitch. He emphasized his words with such a reckless handling of his old shooting iron that he left no doubt in the mind of the rival doctor that he meant exactly what he said. The medicine man took the hint and made no more midnight calls upon his unwilling patient. Free from his ministrations, Howitch's arm eventually healed.

Jimmy's mother often employed Quedessa, an Indian woman, to do the washing and other heavy work about the house. Since she was a willing worker and completely trustworthy, Quedessa soon became a well-liked member of the McCurdy household.

Quedessa's baby, of whom she was inordinately fond, contracted a severe case of croup while Doctor Howell was absent from the reservation. Having learned by experience that the treatment administered by the medicine men usually resulted in the death of their small patients, she had kept the child's sickness a secret while attempting to treat it herself. But the baby had gradually grown worse until one night, in desperation, Quedessa came to Mrs. McCurdy and implored her help in ministering to the desperately sick child.

The white mother's heart went out in sympathy to the dark mother in her distress and she wasted no time in accompanying Quedessa to her house, which was the cleanest and best furnished of the Indian colony. She found the baby in very serious condition and on the verge of choking to death.

Mrs. McCurdy remained at the bedside of the tiny patient all night, employing all the skill and gentleness she had learned in caring for her own children. Doctor Howell could well have been proud of her, for she was able to relieve the Indian baby's suffering and bring it through the crisis. But since the doctor was not there, she continued her homespun treatment from day to day until the child had completely recovered.

The gratitude of Quedessa and her husband, Lighthouse Jack, knew no bounds. These simple people tried by every means they had to show their appreciation, and many a fine salmon or basket of wild berries found its way into the kitchen of their friend in need.

Best of all, Lighthouse Jack, known as one of the most trustworthy of the Indians and one of the tribe's greatest boatmen and hunters, took Jimmy under his wing. As a result, this small white boy was to learn at first hand the inner workings of a primitive civilization which was, even then, fast waning and marked for early extinction.

Jimmy was also interested in the beautiful basket work done by Quedessa and he received a more intimate knowledge of that art than fell to the lot of the average frontier dweller. The gentle-faced Indian woman showed him how the selected marsh grass, gathered at Lake Osette, thirty miles south of the village, was soaked, dried in the sun and finally woven into various shapes. She explained how the coarser baskets and mats were made from long, pliable roots, some even being woven while held under water. To demonstrate her skill she filled one of the larger baskets with water. Jimmy watched it critically to see how many leaks developed, but none appeared.

"How long will it be before it begins to leak?" he finally asked.

"That kind never leak," was Quedessa's proud reply.

She went on to explain that, before the white men came with their metal utensils, all food was cooked in these watertight baskets. The cooking basket was filled with water into which heated stones were placed. The boiling water was then poured into a second basket containing the food. This painstaking operation was continued until the food was cooked . . . at least to the taste of a hungry Indian family. Although her people had always used wooden trenchers, ladles and bowls, as well as a rude kind of mortar and pestle for grinding food, they had never learned the art of making utensils of earthenware or stone to be used over a fire.

Quedessa also confided to Jimmy the secret recipes for

making the permanent dyes used by the older Indian women in their basket-making; a secret not freely imparted to strangers. The boy learned by heart the formulas she gave him.[2]

Through Quedessa's intercession, Attlu and Young Doctor, skilled native carvers, allowed Jimmy to sit beside them while they worked. He never tired of watching Attlu fashion an ornate bracelet or breastpin from a silver dollar, or transform a spruce knot into a warclub so beautifully carved that Jimmy felt it would almost be an honor to receive a crack over the head with it. Attlu wore with great pride upon his own breast a large silver medal which had been presented to him by the Canadian government for proficiency in wood and metal carving.

Young Doctor worked entirely in wood. His output was constructed on broad lines and consisted of totems, large and small[3], thunderbirds at rest and with outstretched wings, headmasks and fishing canoes.

Canoe making, Jimmy decided, was the finest of Young Doctor's skills, although it was such slow and painstaking work that he sometimes lost interest and wandered away to other strange sights and sounds and smells. But he always returned, sooner or later, to the canoe making place on the beach.

2Quedessa's secret color formulas, used in Indian basketry before the coming of commercial dyes and genuine Japanese-manufactured "Indian Baskets" were as follows:
    Red—From the boiled bark of the alder tree
    Green—From the roots of the wild cherry
    Yellow—From ashes and grease melted together
    Blue—From a rare blue clay
    White—Considered as a natural color and never compounded.

3Most anthropologists and historians insist that no Indian tribes inhabiting what is now the state of Washington carved totem poles, which are generally considered to have been peculiar to the Indian cultures of Alaska and British Columbia. Obviously the Makahs, in 1877, were proving that even an anthropologist can be wrong.

CHAPTER FIVE

Canoe Building

A few of the books in the McCurdy family library contained stories of Indians, but Jimmy early decided that those
who wrote them hadn't known what they were talking about.
The Indian canoes of the books were frail affairs of birchbark,
but the ones he watched Young Doctor build were deep-sea
craft, hewn from great cedar logs as much as fifty feet long.

The canoe of the Northwest Indian was as important to
him as was the horse to his brethren of the plains, for without
it he would have starved. And no flimsy affair of birchbark
could contend with the great, gray rollers of the North Pacific
or even the less violent seas of Juan de Fuca Strait. Their canoes
were kin to the sharp-prowed long ships of the Vikings.

Few men could make a canoe well and it was conceded
that none could match the precise skill of Young Doctor, who
had learned his craft from his father who, in turn, had been
taught by his father and so one from time immemorial. It was
also agreed, by the older members of the tribe at any rate, that
Young Doctor had inherited spirit helpers as well as skill from
his ancestors.

The first and most important step in canoe building, Jimmy
learned, was the choosing of a cedar log which was the right
length for the job on hand and of even thickness without limbs
or knots. For the big seagoing canoes used by the Makahs in
hunting whale and seal, this meant a truly giant tree.

The canoe was made from half the log, split lengthwise
and roughly shaped and hollowed out by splitting off slabs with
stone wedges. Sometimes Young Doctor let other Indians help
with this rough work and when he was feeling particularly good
he even taught Jimmy to handle the primitive tools of the canoe
making trade. But when it came to the fine work, done by patient
charring with fire and delicate hacking off of charcoal with
hand-made adze, Young Doctor would allow no hand but his
town to touch the log.

Jimmy, who had heard his father talk of the careful meas-
uring and close precision required in building a ship, was

amazed at the methods of Young Doctor. Perhaps, he decided, the old Indians were right when they said that sea spirits guided the canoe builder's eye and hand, for Young Doctor measured entirely by eye until the dugout was nearing its final shape. Then he bored holes through its sides at intervals and thrust sticks through to gauge the thickness. Later, when the canoe was ready for launching, he plugged these holes with pieces of cedar which would swell tight and waterproof.

The log must, of course, be shaped and curved; not merely hollowed out, and for this the builder used the same method employed by the women in cooking food before the white traders brought metal pots and pans. The canoe was filled with water and hot stones were dropped in. Sometimes, if the craft was to be a large one and the log had excess thickness, he built a fire under it as well, and between the two sources of heat the wood was steamed until it was soft and pliable.

Meantime Young Doctor cut stout pieces of yew or spruce, each piece just the width of the canoe was to have at various points along its length. At the center it would have to be much wider than the original log, while the ends must taper gracefully. These sticks he wedged tightly between the gunwales, like seats in a rowboat, to keep the pliable sides bulging outward. Then he dipped out the water and allowed the canoe to dry in its curved shape. Finally the thwarts were made fast to the canoe's sides by cedar-bark lashings passed through holes bored in thwart and gunwale.

The inside of the canoe was usually painted red with a kind of oil paint made by mixing dye with seal or whale oil. The outside was carefully smoothed with sharkskin (Young Doctor scornfully ignored the suggestion of Jimmy's father that he substitute modern sandpaper for this traditional material); then lightly charred with a cedar bark torch which singed off any remaining roughness and left the hull a handsome black color.

The true secret of the beauty of Young Doctor's finished canoes, Jimmy found, were the curved and ornately carved projections at bow and stern, which the builder fashioned separately, with loving care, and attached with wooden pegs to the almost finished craft. Usually he carved the bow-piece in the shape of an animal's head or the replica of that whale-killing bird of Indian mythology, Thunderbird.

These added pieces gave the canoe the look of a living creature and the Indians said it was "like a salmon . . . flat and wide in the middle, tapering and curving up at both ends." Certainly the splendid canoes of Young Doctor took to the Pacific ocean rollers with all the grace and competence of that great fish.

Attlu was the tribe's expert paddle-maker, fashioning these tools of the Indian boatman's trade from carefully chosen maple wood. Jimmy never tired of watching him etch the stout wood with the traditional designs so old that their meanings were half lost in the mists of time and old men's legends. Some of the paddles were pointed at the blade end so they could be driven into a sandy beach to hold the canoe; others had notched blades to hold a rope when a canoe was being towed.

Everything about the Makah's seagoing canoes had both usefulness and beauty and it pleased Jimmy that even his practical State of Maine father was aware that they were something out of the ordinary. He overheard William McCurdy discussing Young Doctor's latest masterpiece with Captain Libby of the Port Townsend steamboat on the beach one afternoon.

"I've no doubt you've taken note of the hull lines the backward natives have developed on those craft of theirs," he asked the captain.

"I have indeed," the captain had replied, "and it's truly amazing. A hollowed-out cedar log ought to be a clumsy thing, but their canoes are near perfect models of the most advanced clipper ships . . . long, clean run, hollow entrance, beautiful shear . . . everything."

The Boston-trained shipbuilder smiled. "That's right. They were building clipper hulls a thousand years before McKay or Webb, no doubt. Maybe it proves the virtue of laziness; clipper lines make smooth and easy paddling, so they adopted them."

Then he pointed to the carved figure of the thunderbird crowning the highswept prow. "But that shows the futility of generalities," he admitted. "A figure-head's about the only thing on a sailing ship that's not functional, yet they have them too. There's only one reason I know of for taking the time and trouble to carve a figure-head. It gives a touch of beauty to a thing that's made to do a job of work, which don't fit in with my theory on laziness."

Jimmy liked the Indians' theory that sea spirits had a hand in designing their canoes better than his father's practical observations on the evolution of hull design. Certainly they looked like living things when they swept out to sea, propelled by the strong, brown arms of the Makah whalers. And even drawn up on the village beach and covered with mats to protect them from the sun, there was an air of mystery and excitement about them.

CHAPTER SIX

You Can't Get Away from School

A government school for the Makah Indian children was located at Bahada, although the older Indians could see no need for such an institution and regarded it with open hostility. Could they have had their way, its existence would have been brief, a feeling which was shared by the McCurdy boys, who were enrolled as a reluctant minority in this, the only educational institution on Neah Bay.

Jimmy and his brothers objected to the school because its opening put an end to their carefree summer of exploration and adventure, but to the older Indians it represented a dangerous encroachment of white civilization into their tribal ways. These members of an earlier generation had gained their knowledge in the hard school of experience in many practical things. They watched as closely as a broker his ticker tape the price relationship of sealskins to blankets; of salmon to hardtack, molasses and calico. Aside from this, the sea supplied almost all their needs, so why this foolish waste of time with books and slates?

They would much rather have had their children remain under their own tutelage . . . the boys to be taught to hunt, fish and handle canoes; the girls to become proficient in beadwork, basketry and the curing of fish and berries.

The government officials sought to counteract this parental hostility by keeping the children completely away from family influence during the school term. For this purpose two large dormitories had been erected, one for girls and one for boys, and here at least a hundred Indian pupils were fed, lodged and clothed at government expense. Six teachers and two matrons were in charge of the school and the adjoining dormitories.

The white settlers, having long ago found it almost impossible to pronounce the gutterals of Indian proper names, had adopted the expedient of renaming individual natives after well-known characters of history and literature. So at the boarding school on Neah Bay it was not unusual to find U. S. Grant, Jeff Davis and Abe Lincoln sitting at the same table in perfect harmony, while Washington, Colfax, Irving, Jackson and Scott might form another group. Among the girls could be found such celebrities as Martha Washington, Queen Esther, Anne Boleyn, Florence Nightingale, Queen Anne and Minnehaha.

The school itself was a large barnlike structure with but little equipment, for the Indian Department shunned any tendency toward "frills" in the education of its charges. The teachers' desks were true antiques, having long since served out their terms of usefulness in various offices at Washington. The children's desks and benches had been made by various carpenters and embodied the individual ideas of the builders with no attempt at uniformity. The blackboards were of huge smoothed planks coated with a dull-finish paint or slating.

On the unpainted walls hung an ancient map of the United States and another of Washington Territory. The latter map, though of generous size, had omitted little Waadah Island at the mouth of Neah Bay. This glaring oversight cast grave doubts on the authenticity of all maps as far as Jimmy and his Indian schoolmates were concerned. How could you trust a map-maker who didn't know about the most important island in the world . . . the one right in your front yard?

One of the older pupils had tried to remedy this omission by sketching in the island with colored crayons. No attempt had been made to conform to scale, however, and the tiny islet appeared ridiculously large compared to Vancouver Island, which loomed along the northern horizon across the twenty-mile stretch of water which formed the international boundary line between the United States and British Columbia.

The artistic license involved in the Washington Territory map seemed reasonable to Jimmy, for was not little Waadah just as completely an island as Vancouver, Ceylon or Madagascar? He had circumnavigated it many times in the canoe of Lighthouse Jack and had explored it thoroughly. Increase tiny Waadah to the size of those other great islands and its Lookout Hill would become a mighty mountain, its Salmon Creek would vie with the Columbia River and its Old Doctor's Cove would become another San Francisco Bay, but, Jimmy decided, he wouldn't like it as well or know it as intimately. Besides, he learned, mere size can be a disadvantage. Australia, the geography teacher pointed out, had been forced to relinquish the distinction of being the world's biggest island and had become just another continent.

Austere as it was, the Neah Bay Indian School had the distinction of being one of the first schools in the United States to promote manual arts and home economics for its Indian students. Classes in agriculture, carpentry and blacksmithing were offered to the boys; cooking and sewing to the girls.

The Indian children proved generally adept at these practical subjects, but they were slow at "book learning." Some of the younger pupils even had to be taught to speak English. Indian Agent Walton, whose children were also enrolled at the Indian School, agreed with Jimmy's parents that a course of study geared to the needs of Makah children was not well suited for white children who would some day face the need of making a living in more civilized regions.

To make matters worse, Doctor Howell discovered symptoms of tuberculosis among a number of the older Indian children. Little was known about the dreaded "white plague" in those days . . . except that it was incurable and deadly. As a result of the doctor's fearful discovery, Bill, Jimmy, Frank and Agent Walton's three children became part of the little group of white children at Neah Bay receiving no schooling whatever.

This development was fine with Jimmy, but it was a matter of much concern to the white parents of the colony. In addition to the five who had been attending the Indian School, the juvenile population of white Neah Bay included blacksmith Thad Warren's four lusty boys, the three Fisher children, whose father was in charge of the reservation farm, and two in the family of Fred Matheson, keeper of the government lifesaving station.

A total of 14 children certainly justified a school, the parents decided, and the result was a unanimous vote to hire a teacher for an eight months term, each family to share a portion of the expense. Agent Walton volunteered the use of his government-furnished conveyance, an ancient one-horse rig, to serve as village school bus.

It was soon discovered that not many teachers were enthusiastic about spending eight dreary, rain-soaked winter months in such an isolated place, but a courageous lady named Alice Winters was at last induced to sign up for the position.

The new teacher was tall and spare with grey-touched brown hair parted in the exact center and brushed back uncompromisingly to a prim bun in back. Her keen black eyes, which seemed to overlook nothing within her range of vision, were reinforced by a pair of steel-rimmed spectacles. Her lips, naturally thin, had been kept closely compressed for so long that they no longer possessed any semblance of a curve. This pattern seemed to have been followed throughout in the creation of Miss Winters for she was, as Jimmy's shipbuilder father admitted dryly, "constructed along angular lines." The unvarying uniform of Miss Winters was a sober black dress with no nonsense about it except for a dash of snowy white at neck and wrists.

Jimmy's father made a serviceable teacher's desk fitted with shelves and drawers, individual desks and benches for the pupils and a blackboard. These, together with an old box stove, a water bucket and tin dipper, comprised the equipment that was assembled in a room of the rambling structure which bore the imposing title of Government Building. In this improvised school room the fourteen white children of Neah Bay, ranging in age from six to fourteen years, took up their simple studies under the watchful eye of Miss Winters.

It was well that the teacher was a strict disciplinarian, for the three older boys, Phil Walton, Jack Matheson and Hugo Warren, required a firm hand to hold them in check. They had taken many liberties at the free-and-easy Indian School and they proposed to continue the same tactics with Miss Winters. Phil was the leader among the boys, full of mischief and venturesome to the point of rashness. He was inclined to take advantage of the fact that he was the Indian Agent's son and had kept the school at Bahada in almost constant turmoil. The teachers there were overjoyed to learn they were no longer to be favored with his presence.

In order to annoy Miss Winters, Phil made use of a disagreeable trick with which he had enjoyed much success at the Indian school. On the way to classes he would fill his pockets with wild garlic, which he would chew slyly throughout the day. The resulting scent would never be mistaken for attar of roses and the other pupils registered a strong protest against being required to breathe air which, they claimed, they could actually taste.

After enduring this nuisance for a brief period, Miss Winters grimly produced a cake of strong yellow soap and a brush, with which she proceeded to thoroughly wash out the offender's mouth. Phil was a brave and determined boy, but Miss Winters was too much for him. Just two of these treatments were sufficient to cause the garlic eater to lose his fondness for the odiferous little plant.

The boys refused to give up without a further struggle, however. The water bucket, sitting in a corner of the school room, was renewed each morning by one of the boys, whose duty it was to fill it at the pump outside. On two occasions Hugo Warren, while assigned to this duty, contrived to stub his toe spectacularly on the doorsill and send the water cascading all over the floor. Upon the second occurrence it was plain to Miss Winters that Hugo's accidents were premeditated.

"This is an excellent time to give the room a much needed scrubbing, Hugo," she said sweetly, "and see that you do a good job while you are about it."

Forthwith she set the culprit to mopping up the water with a piece of sacking. Hugo was a plump boy and the combination of bending and hard exercise was a strain upon both his too-small trousers and his limited wind, but whenever he showed signs of lagging the implacable Miss Winters stimulated his efforts by the application of a stout switch to the tightly stretched seat of his trousers. By the time the job was completed to her satisfaction, poor Hugo had transferred a goodly portion of the water to his own person and was much chastened and subdued.

Jack Matheson, the third member of the troublesome trio, was the owner of a mongrel puppy which had a habit of pawing its ear, at the same time giving vent to a series of plaintive and comical whines. Jack had become quite proficient at imitating his dog's performance, an act which never failed to evoke much laughter from his audience. He was foolish enough to start his ear-stroking act in school one day and soon had the class snickering. Miss Winters ignored the disturbance until the amateur comedian was through, a fact which should have aroused his suspicions had his brain been as well developed as his talent.

As Jack returned to his books, well satisfied with his dramatic triumph, Miss Winters took a hand.

"Keep right on, Jack," she commanded. "And as your friends seem to be enjoying the performance, just come up here in front where they can all see you."

Jack complied with rather poor grace. His ear, under the continued stroking, began to throb and the exhibition ceased to amuse him. But when he evinced a desire to stop Miss Winters stood ready to give him a cut across the legs with her switch, compelling him to keep on until his ear was badly swollen and his ego badly shrunken.

"You may stop now, Jack," Miss Winters said primly, "but I give you fair warning if you start playing puppy in school again your act will have a longer run."

Thus did the terrible Miss Winters subdue the last of the persistent disturbers of the peace and harmony of Neah Bay school.

CHAPTER SEVEN

Jimmy Speaks a Piece

On Friday afternoons, following the established custom of one-room schools the nation over, the pupils of the Neah Bay white school "spoke pieces" and school was dismissed an hour earlier than usual. Although most of the pupils professed to hate these exercises, Jimmy rather enjoyed them and readily took part, for he had not reached the self-conscious age and could memorize easily.

Miss Winters, perhaps rather unwisely, had made frequent public commendations of Jimmy's reciting ability, intimating that the others might well follow his example. Her remarks, of course, tended to create resentment in the minds of Phil, Jack and Hugo, who had received more punishment than praise from her. They began to plot a method of undermining Jimmy's reputation as an orator.

"What are you going to speak this afternoon, Jimmy?" asked Phil casually on a certain Friday afternoon.

"I've got three pieces ready, but I don't know yet which one I'll use," Jimmy answered innocently.

"Three!" Phil affected great admiration. "You're sure a smart kid. What are they?"

Still unsuspicious, Jimmy replied, "Let's see . . . there's *Twinkle, Twinkle, Little Star* and *Down Silver Lake* and that one about the Great White Owl in the reader."

He was soon to regret this confidence.

It was Miss Winter's custom to call first upon the older pupils first, and Phil responded with the well known classic which he had changed to suit himself, beginning:

> "Twinkle, twinkle, little star,
> How I wonder what you are;
> Keep your place up in the sky,
> For if you fall it means goodbye."

Miss Winters frowned and Jimmy gasped in astonishment as he listened to this revised version of the prize selection of his limited repertoire.

Miss Winters wasn't amused either. "That's a rather childish piece for a boy your age," she informed the grinning Phil, "and I don't think you have improved it a bit."

Poor Jimmy's consternation was great indeed when Jack took his place before the class to take liberties with another of the selections he had in reserve:

> "When I went down to Silver Lake
> I met a little rattlesnake;
> He ate so much of jelly cake
> It made his little belly ache."

Miss Winters again frowned her disapproval, but made no formal comment. As for trusting Jimmy, he was thrown into a panic when, with two of his prepared numbers gone, plump Hugo assayed to recite *The Great White Owl*. Not having had time to memorize it properly, Hugo was a long time staggering through it and was in obvious dread of Miss Winters' switch. Everyone but Jimmy breathed more freely when, by dint of much prompting and perspiration, Hugo reached the end.

"That owl must have been very patient, as well as wise," Miss Winters commented dryly, "or it would have flown away long before you finished your oration." Then she turned to Jimmy. "It's your turn now. I'm glad we can always depend upon you to contribute something worth while to our program."

Jimmy stood amazed and practically speechless at the perfidy of the conspirators who had so brazenly appropriated his three selections. He had been thinking hard, but in his confused state of mind could recall nothing he had not already recited . . . and no repetitions were permitted. It never occurred to him to turn informer and thus explain the situation.

"I—I haven't got any piece today," he finally stammered.

"Why, Jimmy, you've never failed us before," the teacher exclaimed, hardly able to believe her ears. "It would be too bad now to spoil your record and lose a mark. You must certainly have *some* piece prepared."

Jimmy stood silent as he tried to conjure up some way out of his predicament. His mind seemed to have gone temporarily blank and the poorly suppressed delight of the three conspirators added to his bewilderment.

Miss Winters waited expectantly, refusing to believe that her prize reciter had deliberately flunked out. She felt instinctively that something was wrong, but she still hadn't decided just what it was.

As for Jimmy, he was fast being driven to the point where he might be expected to throw control to the winds and do something unexpected. A wild idea had flashed into his mind, whereby he could avoid the loss of his reputation as a reciter and, at the same time, be avenged upon his tormentors. Even though Miss Winters would be shocked and he himself doubtless suffer punishment, he felt a driving need to carry out his impulse.

Without stopping to further consider his action, he assumed a proper oratorical stance and rattled off in a defiant manner a piece of doggeral which had popped into his mind and remained there to the exclusion of all else of a literary nature:

> "When the American Eagle flew south,
> He caught Miss Winters up in his mouth;
> But when he found he had a fool,
> He dropped her into the Neah Bay school.
>
> Yes, here he dropped her mighty quick,
> And thought he done a clever trick;
> We hope he'll come again some day,
> And take her off . . . then hip hurray!"

Had the sturdy old stove blown up and scattered its fragments about the room, it could scarcely have caused greater consternation, for even poor Jimmy could hardly believe the words were coming out of his own mouth. Miss Winters' registered profound amazement mixed with indignation, while the smug satisfaction of the three plotters changed to abject alarm.

"Why Jimmy McCurdy! What do you mean by speaking a piece like that?" the teacher demand when she had recovered somewhat from her first shock.

Jimmy, apalled at what he had done, tried to dig a hole in the schoolroom's plank floor with one copper-toed boot. "You kept nagging me so I had to speak something," he muttered. "That piece got stuck in my mind and I had to let it come out."

"Where did you learn such a perfect gem of poetry?" the teacher asked sarcastically.

"Phil made it up and Jack and Hugo kept saying it so often that I learned it by heart," Jimmy admitted.

"I thought so. I'm very much surprised that you would speak such a piece before my very face and you ought to be punished for it, but it's just as well I know how these boys regard me." Miss Winters tapped the desk with her ruler. "The time is up and school is dismissed. Phil, Jack, Hugo . . . and Jimmy . . . you will remain."

The pupils filed out, silent and orderly, which was unusual for a Friday afternoon release from discipline. The culprits, filled with vague apprehension, huddled together staring at the teacher and wondering what dire punishment would be meted out to them. The joke on Jimmy had proved a boomerang indeed.

For some minutes Miss Winters remained silent. For all her intrepid and uncompromising air, she had found this last outpost of civilization with its pungent smells, restricted activities and continuous gloom almost more than she could stand.

Working with a handful of children in a drab, one-room school had seemed so futile and uninspiring that she had found herself wondering if she could serve out the term.

The humiliation of this afternoon had been the final blow to the lonely teacher and the result was as strange to the boys as it was unexpected. Staid, stern, self-reliant Miss Winters, covering her face with her handkerchief and weeping bitterly!

The boys glanced at each other guiltily. They had never imagined anything as awful as this. The worst punishment that could have been visited upon them would have been far better. Jimmy tried hard not to join Miss Winters in her grief, but he felt a strong urge to set up a caterwauling that would drown out her muffled sobs. He couldn't remember ever having felt worse since he was a baby in Port Townsend and was so sick he nearly died.

Presently the teacher dried her eyes and said, with a tremor in her usually stern voice, "Boys, remember I did not need to take this position. I came because I was told I was needed here. I've tried to keep a good school and get you all started in the right direction. I don't mind a little mischief. I'm used to that, but I didn't realize until now that you children hate me and would be pleased if you could drive me away. By humiliating me before the whole school you got what you wanted because I am going to give up the school at once."

Phil carried beneath an undeniably rough exterior a warm heart, and was always ready to acknowledge a fault. Without a moment's hesitation he rose from his seat and burst out impetuously:

"Please don't feel bad, Miss Winters. I didn't mean to hurt your feelings. I took most of that piece out of a boys' book and put your name in just to make the kids laugh. We all like you a lot and we don't want you to leave. You know how to manage us and make us learn. And don't blame Jimmy either, because we put him in a bad spot and he took the only way out he could find."

Having started, Phil went on to tell about the plot they had entered into in order to "take Jimmy down a peg or two." His frank explanation was so convincing and was so ably backed up by Jack and Hugo that Miss Winters accepted it at its full value. Then, as its ludicrous aspects struck her, a warm smile erased the stern lines from her mouth. Jimmy was more amazed than ever. With her steel-rimmed spectacles forgotten on the desk, her eyes softened by tears and her mouth by that bright smile, Miss Winters was downright pretty!

That was the end of the warfare at the Neah Bay school. Miss Winters finished that term and signed up for another, but that one was never completed; probably because she kept forgetting to wear her steel-rimmed spectacles and seemed to have gotten into the habit of smiling. Before the term was over she had married the chief engineer of the government lighthouse tender *Manzanita* whom she met on the beach at Neah Bay.

When she sailed away on the steamboat *Libby* to a home in Seattle provided by her brand new husband, who had a blue uniform, brass buttons and a properly heroic mustache, Jimmy stood on the beach feeling strangely lonely and waving goodbye until the *Libby* rounded the point and left only a tattered banner of smoke behind in Neah Bay.

Jimmy hoped that Miss Winters would live happily ever after, and he was quite certain that she would.

CHAPTER EIGHT

Unbidden Guests at a Kloqually Dance

"I want you boys to stick pretty close to home for the next few days," Mr. McCurdy told his sons one August morning following the ending of the first year's school term at Neah Bay. "The Indians are going to hold a Kloqually and there is no telling what they might do after being stirred up by their old witch doctors."

No further explanation was given, nor was it necessary, for the boys had learned through observation what a Kloqually was. They were well aware that it was the annual war dance of the Makahs and would last for several days.

They likewise knew that during the celebration the men would cut themselves and smear blood over the faces of the women and children. Then, attired in war paint and grotesque costumes, they would go racing up and down the beach yelling and giving all indications of having reverted to complete savagery . . . as, in reality, they had for the time being.

The occasion would also be utilized to mete out punishments to such tribesmen as had violated any traditional laws of the Makahs and it was generally understood that an Indian known as Black Frank was to be the principal object of vengeance this year. He was a treacherous, quarrelsome and dishonest individual, detested by whites and natives alike.

Black Frank had been found guilty of neglecting and abusing his family, but that might have been overlooked by the usually tolerant Makahs; he had stolen and sold several canoes, which was a more serious offense, but might still have been forgiven in the course of time. He was, however, an arrant coward and had shrunk from the ordeal of being slashed for the Kloqually festivities and this was the act that had filled his fellow tribesmen with righteous indignation and called for rigorous punishment.

Well aware of his unpopularity and of what was probably in store for him, Black Frank had departed the village and hidden away in the dense rain forest inland, but he was tracked down and dragged unceremoniously before the council. In

69

accordance with its verdict, he was cut more artistically and deeper than was ordinarily done and, as a final touch, slits were cut in the flesh of each flank. Through these slits, fish-lines were passed and the culprit was driven along the beach tandem-fashion by the chief, as an example to any who might be considering defiance of tribal regulations. The women and children mocked him and threw sand upon his bleeding body.

With their appetite for excitement properly whetted, the Makahs proposed to gather that night in one of the huge cedar lodges to enjoy traditional bursts of oratory, war dancing, spear throwing and other feats of strength and agility. Few if any white persons had ever attended a Kloqually night session and it was something of a mystery as to just what took place behind the guarded doors.

While the Kloqually was still in session, Jack Walton held a secret conference with the McCurdy boys. "No white boy on this reservation has ever found what goes on in the Kloqually house and I'm determined to find out," he announced. "I've got it all figured out and I've already got permission to stay with you tonight so we can go early and hide in the Kloqually house and see everything that goes on."

"What if we get caught?" asked Bill. Jimmy felt his brother's question was a good one, but he was determined to take his cue from the two older boys.

"There ain't much chance of that," Jack said confidently. "Anyway, they wouldn't dare touch me 'cause I'm the agent's son and they're mighty careful how they treat men. I'd protect you . . . so there ain't nothing to be scared of."

Jack's cogent arguments and the strong urge of curiosity won the McCurdy brothers over and that evening, while the meeting place was still deserted, they crept in and hid behind a large black box standing in a corner near a door. Here they felt relatively safe and could see without being seen.

The windowless chamber was lit eerily by the dim light of lanterns salvaged from wrecked ships by the Indians; red, green and white. Several fires were burning upon the well-swept earthen floor and great spruce knots were blazing in the dark corners. The leaping flames, choking smoke and shifting shadows reminded Jimmy of a woodcut in one of the volumes of the family library . . . Dante's *Inferno*.

The boys had hardly become settled in their hiding place when in trooped a number of scantily clad participants, their faces daubed barbarically with red and black paint; the whites of their eyes and fang-like teeth gleaming weirdly in the subdued and flickering light. Others kept streaming in until the cavernous room was well filled. Among the later arrivals were a number of natives who were to take no part in the ceremonies and sat upon the sidelines as interested spectators.

To the music of a horse-hide drum, the clatter of rattles

and a montonous chanting, a free-for-all dance opened the evening's festivities. This continued with ever-increasing fervor until the dancers were in a frenzy and almost ready to drop from exhaustion.

When quiet was finally restored, one of the tribal elders began an extended harangue designed to incite the performers to even greater efforts. Under the lash of his impassioned oratory the wild dance resumed with savage variations. Several of the dancers scooped up handsfull of glowing coals from the fires and, heaping them upon their bushy heads, kept them in place with their bare hands until the room was filled with the smell of burning hair.

Other hardy souls danced with mantles of stinging nettles draped about their otherwise naked bodies, their frenzied movements indicating that the nettles had not lost their efficiency. One actor, painted to represent a wild animal, climbed to an overhead platform and began pelting the crowd below with the miscellaneous articles stored on the rafters and hanging from the ceiling. A sack nearly filled with flour was included in the barrage, being emptied on the celebrants in handsfulls until everyone present had received a baptism of flour.

Meanwhile, gourds of whale oil were periodically thrown upon the fires, causing them to flare up with a mysterious lustre and giving the frenzied movements of the Indians the effect of barbaric tableaux.

So entranced were the white boys that they hardly noticed the sudden loud command of the chief until it was answered by a concerted rush upon the large black box behind which they were crouched. Before they could make a movement the box was dragged out of the corner, disclosing the four startled youngsters to the equally surprised gaze of the Indians.

The boys were unceremoniously hustled out into the center of the room amid a great clamor, where they were placed under the guard of several villainous-looking warriors armed with madrona-wood clubs. Many dark looks were directed at the interlopers and it was obvious that Jack's confidence in his personal safety was not as complete as it had been earlier that day.

As for the Indians, the situation was unprecedented and offered a difficult problem for solution. Here were four individuals caught spying upon their secret rites and ceremonies, but they were only boys . . . and one of them was the agent's son. How were they to be dealt with?

The old chief kept the boys in suspense for some time while he held a heated pow-wow with his braves. The Northwest Indians were not without a sense of humor, although the point of a joke was often slow to dawn upon them. Fortunately, the amusing side of the situation finally appealed to the old Makah and he voiced his decision; the culprits would escape punishment, but they must be made members of the tribe by an appropriate ceremony.

Accordingly the boys were stood in a row and a hideously masked medicine man approached them with a blood-letting knife, its thin blade flickering in the firelight. Jimmy gritted his teeth manfully, determined not to show a trace of weakness.

He and his fellow conspirators each received a light knife-prick just deep enough to draw a drop or two of blood, which was smeared upon their cheeks and foreheads. Some flour was then scraped up from the floor and sprinkled on their heads, after which they were required to take several puffs on a long ceremonial pipe, given an oath of secrecy and declared members of the Makah tribe.

This ceremony was conducted with the utmost gravity and upon its completion the initiates were given seats with the other spectators, being first cautioned to maintain absolute silence. Filled with a mixture of fright, relief and pride, the boys, for once, observed that admonition to the letter.

From the black box which had been their hiding place a number of carved wooden head masks were now withdrawn. These were helmet-shaped and fitted over the heads of the wearers, completely disguising their appearance. Some represented animals with great, staring eyes, white teeth and pointed snouts; others resembled birds with long, curved bills. All were painted in vivid colors and, as the wearers pranced about brandishing weapons, the effect was bizarre and frightening, especially to the four most recently initiated members of the tribe.

The mask wearers were knife throwers and skilled spearsmen. With blood-curdling screeches they would thrust their keen weapons within a few inches of the spectators' faces or hurl them through the crowd into the wall, there to remain quivering. Their antics finished the Kloqually festivities. The whale oil had been used up, the torches had been extinguished and the fires had burned low.

Among the first to emerge from that eerie place were the four boys, nor did they loiter long in the vicinity.

"Now ain't you glad you came?" asked Jack triumphantly, after they had placed a safe distance between themselves and the Kloqually house. "I'll bet we're the only boys in the whole world that ever saw a real war dance, and we're members of the tribe, too!"

"I was awful scared when that medicine man came at me with his knife," Jimmy admitted, "and when they got to throwing those spears. One almost pinned my ear to the wall. But I'm glad now we went."

The night was still young and the boys' absence had not occasioned any alarm, so they carefully removed their shoes, sneaked into the kitchen, washed the dried blood and flour off their faces and tip-toed to bed.

72

In the face of the warning they had received, they felt duty bound not to mention having been at the Kloqually dance or to disclose what they had seen there. The Indians, however, were not so discreet. They thought the joke was too good to be kept secret and before long the whole story reached the ears of the boys' parents.

Jimmy, Bill and Frank then underwent a woodshed conference with their father which was more painful than their initiation into the Makah tribe. But they agreed afterward that the adventure had been well worth the price.[4]

---

[4]The boys were probably right, because the Makah Kloqually ceremonies became progressively more secretive in the following years. Indian agents were much opposed to the ceremony, believing it helped keep alive the spirit of savagery in the minds of the natives. Shortly after the incident described here the Department of Indian Affairs published an order forbidding Kloqually dances. The Makahs refused to obey the order, and for years continued to hold their dances secretly at some remote part of the reservation. In time the custom became obsolete.

CHAPTER NINE

Potlatch

Not long after the Kloqually observance the Makahs held another celebration of an entirely different nature. Known as *Potlatch*,[5] this was a time devoted to good fellowship and the presentation of gifts. It was, like the white man's Christmas, a custom of great antiquity. Perhaps before the coming of the Christ Child brought Christmas into the world the Northwest Indians were observing the gift-giving festival of Potlatch.

The Potlatch opened in colorful style with a grand parade along the beach, in which both tribes took part. The participants were clad in picturesque costumes of gay colors embellished with feathers, shells and beadwork. The Canadian Indians wore strings of beads made from the slender white tusk-shaped dentalium shell, which they fished up from the Vancouver Island coast. These shells were used for money and a necklace long enough to hang to the knees was a sign of wealth and a source of great pride to its wearer. Many of the dancers wore ornaments of polished abalone shell inserted in holes through their noses and all were well daubed with paint for the festive occasion.

The parade was followed by a spirited canoe race between the two tribes, the course being to Bahada Point and back. Three canoes from each tribe competed, each manned by eight paddlers and a helmsman. The canoes were not of the narrow racing variety, but ordinary sturdy craft such as were used in the whaling and sealing expeditions. As a preliminary, how-

---

[5]George Shaw, student of early Indian lore and author of an authoritative dictionary of the Chinook jargon, described the Potlatch as follows: "A present or gift; expecting no return; a donation. The Potlatch was the greatest institution of the Indians * * * From far and near assembled the invited guests and tribes and with feasting, singing, chanting and dancing, the bounteous collection was distributed. A chief was made penniless, the wealth of a lifetime was dissipated in an hour, but his head ever after was crowned with the glory of a satisfied ambition; he had won the reverence and honor of his people. It was a beautiful custom; beautiful in the eyes of the natives of high or low degree."

Other authorities disagreed, however. Indian Agent Debeck, of Alert Bay in 1906 charged the Potlatch "is at the bottom of all evils besetting the Indians", adding that it had degenerated into a market for the selling of slaves and an excuse for protracted gambling orgies.

Like the Kloqually, the Potlatch has become an almost forgotten rite among the Pacific Northwest Indians.

ever, the hulls of the canoes were carefully gone over with strips of burning cedar bark to remove any splinters, much as a turkey is singed to get rid of the pin feathers. Next came a thorough rubbing with whale oil to reduce friction.

The contestants proved to be very evenly matched and excitement ran high. As the racers came knifing down the homeward stretch, their paddles rising and falling in perfect unison, two canoes gradually drew away from the others to near the winning post in a dashing neck and neck finish . . . a King George canoe and a Makah.

A few yards from the finish line came a crash and two paddlers in the Makah craft went tumbling backward upon those behind ,throwing the crew into wild disorder. The King George canoe swept grandly across the finish line to be declared the winner.

The decision was hotly contested by the losing crew and their supporters, many of whom had wagered heavily on their favorite canoe. A thwart had broken loose from its fastenings, an unheard of weakness in a craft built by Young Doctor, and there were muttered charges that it was no accident, but the result of tampering. The thwart was passed from hand to hand to substantiate the charge and it did appear that the supports had been slashed with a knife.[6] Jimmy and his companions, ardent partisans of their Makah friends, were loud in their protests against this foul play, but the visitors refused to concede the point and for a time it appeared that the joyful Potlatch would break up in a free-for-all fight before it had well begun. But the tribal heads, determined that Makah dignity should be maintained at any cost, intervened to prevent open warfare and the losing team withdrew the charge and lapsed into sulky silence.

Soon the festival crowd forgot its animosities as a loud-voiced Makah sub-chief announced that the Potlatch feast was ready. Dignity cast aside, chiefs and commoners raced for the commodious lodge known as the Potlatch House. Large as it was, the great cedar structure was barely able to accommodate the mob that pushed its way in, sweating and pushing.

The white boys were not greatly tempted by the feast which was served. Salmon, smoked, dried and boiled, was much in evidence, but there were side dishes of octopus stew, boiled potatoes, pilot-bread and blackstrap molasses, all to be washed down with quantities of seal oil. The Indians, however, seized whatever viands were closest at hand and gorged themselves

[6]Such sharp practice was not above the Makah's Nitinat guests, who were noted for their shrewdness where gambling or trading profits were involved. Of an earlier Makah—Nitinat Potlatch, Northwest historian C. T. Conover wrote: "The Nitinat guests from Vancouver Island got most of the plunder—one distinguished trait of these natives is their appreciation of financial values, and in trade these guileless children of nature can see just as far as a white man."

happily without resort to knives or forks. No Indian was ever known to wait for a "second helping."

When the last scraps of food had disappeared came the most popular feature of the Potlatch . . . the distribution of the gifts that were piled high on a platform at one end of the lodge. Blankets, tobacco, raw sugar, pilot-bread, beads, fish-hooks, mirrors and many other articles were dispensed, the gifts being apportioned in close conformity with the social position of the recipients.

At this point the boys, resolving not to be overlooked upon such a gala occasion, pushed their way boldly into the crowded arena and, facing the dispenser of gifts, loudly cried, "Potlatch! Potlatch!" Refusal would be a rank discourtesy and a reflection upon the Potlatch spirit of the tribe, so Jimmy and his white friends were allotted minor gifts of the kind given Makah boys who had not yet assumed the rights of tribal braves.

Not entirely satisfied with what they had received, they returned later and greeted those emerging from the lodge with the magic salutation, "Potlatch!" Here again, custom demanded that gifts should be shared and the boys continued to levy tribute until the Potlatch House was empty. With pockets and blouses stuffed to full capacity, they finally retired from the scene, firmly convinced that Potlatch was the most satisfying celebration ever instituted by any tribe or nation.

In the evening the festivities were renewed at the Potlatch House. Speeches were made, formally welcoming the visitors and extolling the contributors to the Potlatch. Wild native dances and songs served as preliminaries to the main event of the evening, an exhibition by Circus Joe, the Makah's prize performer.

This Indian, when a young boy, had traveled extensively with Barnum's Circus and had learned many of the sideshow performers' tricks. When he returned to the reservation he proudly demonstrated his prowess without revealing to the tribe how his marvels were accomplished. In consequence he was looked upon as possessing "heap powerful medicine" and was viewed with great respect even by those arch-showmen, the witch doctors.

This night Circus Joe stood naked to the waist, his face and body painted with brilliant ochre. The Potlatch visitors grunted their admiration as he rolled a heavy cannonball around his neck and along his arms, whirled a musket around his body with lightning-like rapidity, picked various objects out of space or from the persons of amazed spectators, ate glass and swallowed a long knife, pulled yards of paper out of his mouth and, as a grand finale, breathed out volumes of fire from mouth and nostrils.

His exhibition, as always, won the admiration of the spectators, but left the medicine men, who could perform no such wonders, sulking and envious. Jimmy hoped that if Circus Joe ever got sick he would call upon the services of Doctor Howell and not the medicine men.

Following the formal ceremonies, many of the Indians remained in the Potlatch House for the usual post-Potlatch gambling which would strip many of them of their personal possessions as well as their newly awarded gifts. Jimmy and the other white boys remained, as unobtrusively as possible, at the edge of the crowd watching preparations for the playing of the "stick game."

Large cedar mats were placed on the floor and thirty round cedar sticks carefully counted out and placed on each mat, three rows of five each at each end of the mat with a twelve-inch open space in the center. Twelve gingersnap-sized counters were used, one white, called the "queen." These counters were divided equally and hidden in two balls of cedar shavings.

A dealer placed a ball of shavings with the hidden counters in each hand and began an intricate figure-eight movement of his arms amid a tremendous accompaniment of drums, chants and screams. After five or ten minutes of this, the opposing team leader would point to one hand of the dealer. If this hand held the "queen" the winning team moved one of the cigar-sized sticks to its end of the mat. If the guess was wrong, the dealer's team claimed the stick.

Jimmy concluded that the first side to win all the sticks would claim the game and the growing heap of goods which was being wagered upon it, but before the long-drawn-out ceremony ended, he felt a strong hand upon his arm. Mr. McCurdy had remembered something his sons had forgotten in the excitement of Potlatch; it was long past their bed time. Presumably the inter-tribal "sing gamble" went on all night, but Potlatch was over as far as Jimmy, Bill and Frank were concerned.

The following year the King George Indians proclaimed a Potlatch on Vancouver Island with the Makahs as their guests, but it was claimed the King George Indians had returned the hospitality of the Boston Indians in a most niggardly fashion and the Makahs returned across the strait much dissatisfied with the treatment they had received and the poor quality of the gifts which had been given them.

The boys were likewise much dissastified with this celebration held on foreign soil, as they received no loaves or fishes from that feast.[7]

---

[7]Indian Agent Walton investigated the affair and was so convinced that his wards had been badly fleeced by the sharper British Columbia natives that he put a stop to this international exchange of Potlatch courtesies.

CHAPTER TEN

A Case of Lost Bearings

One Saturday shortly after the Potlatch celebration, Mrs. McCurdy called Frank and Jimmy into the kitchen. "I saw one of the Indians with a basket of huckleberries yesterday," she said. "I know its rather early for them, but if you boys can find some I'll make you a huckleberry pie."

No further inducement was necessary and within minutes the two boys, each carrying a tin pail, were on their way toward one of many forest trails which radiated like wheel-spokes from the dry swamp in back of the village.

"Don't go too far or stay too long," their mother called after them, but the boys were already almost out of sight, Jimmy striving manfully to keep up with his older brother and both driven onward at top speed by visions of the savory berry pie which awaited them if their expedition met with success.

As the boys entered the thick underbrush of the forested rise behind the village they noted that a grey fog bank was hugging the distant Vancouver Island shore and the air above the placid strait was hazy, but the weather was pleasant and the sun filtered brightly through the age-old canopy of spruce and Douglas fir above them. The boys soon found, however, that the Indian their mother had seen with huckleberries had certainly rushed the season or had stumbled upon an early-ripening patch in some especially sunny clearing.

Hoping to find such a spot, the boys wandered further and further into the dense evergreen forest and, with supreme confidence in their ability to retrace their steps, soon ignored the trails entirely. They were encouraged in their search by finding here and there clusters of berries which, although not as plump and blue as they would have liked, were still ripe enough for a pie.

Several hours thus passed, during which they traveled a much greater distance than they realized. So intent had they been upon their berry picking that they had failed to notice a dark bank of clouds which, surmounting the sombre, spruce-clad hills, had gradually covered almost the entire sky. Suddenly the sun was blotted out abruptly, as though covered by a giant hand. The boys, greatly startled, looked up at the lowering sky which seemed suddenly to be pressing against the very tree-tops.

"I'll bet it's going to rain like the dickens," Frank exclaimed.

"And we're a long way from home," Jimmy admitted unhappily, setting down his nearly empty bucket and peering into the unfamiliar forest in search of some comforting familiar landmark.

He had hardly finished speaking when a vivid flash of lightning streaked across the sky, followed by a crash of thunder. Flash succeeded flash and peal followed peal, momentarily lighting up the darkened forest with an unearthly glow. Then from the clouds that seemed to be resting on the tree-tops came a deluge of rain, rattling upon the dry underbrush like a fusillade of buckshot.

The boys scrambled for shelter under a large spruce tree, its dense foliage for a time protecting them like a widespread green umbrella, but soon the water began to seep through even this thick covering, soaking them to the skin.

Deciding that they couldn't possibly get any wetter or more uncomfortable, the boys decided to begin their return journey, but they could find no sign of any trail and the unpleasant realization came to them that they had lost all sense of direction. The lightning had ceased and the thunder had gone rumbling off to be lost in the high solitudes of the Olympic Mountains, but the rain continued with the dreary persistent monotony peculiar to the rain forest country of the far Northwest. Jimmy, in spite of all his determination, could make but slow progress through the dripping undergrowth even with Frank helping him as best he could over the worst places.

After much weary plodding Frank paused to wipe the blood from a cut on his nose caused by a whipping branch of wickedly spiked devil club. "We ought to be getting towards home by this time," he said hopefully.

"If we're going in the right direction," Jimmy added. "Everything looks strange to me. See that little hill over there? I never saw that before."

Frank peered through the sadly falling rain toward the higher ground his brother had pointed out.

"Look," he exclaimed, "there's a big canoe pulled up on the top of that hill. I'll bet we find an Indian house on the other side."

This welcome evidence of human habitation raised the boys' spirits and gave added strength to their chilled bodies, so they made good time toward the canoe-crowned hill. As they climbed the gentle slope and came nearer to the canoe their curiosity was intensified, for in it was an object which stood out lividly against the dark background of weathered cedar.

79

The canoe, it soon became apparent, was so old and rotten that it was only the ghostly ruin of a once graceful Makah dugout. And as the boys pressed nearer they were brought face to face with the mysterious white object which occupied it . . . a bleached skeleton sitting in a crouched position, the skull grinning hideously at them from a tangle of mouldy blankets from which the soaking rain drew a fetid, sickening odor. Fastenings of some kind appeared to be holding the bones in their strange position.

For one horrified instant the boys stared into the face of the ancient corpse and its empty eye-sockets seemed to return their gaze. It is doubtful that they took in any of the minor details of the macabre scene; their one wild-eyed glance had revealed a good deal more than they desired to see.

Impelled by a common impulse, they turned from the dread object in the death canoe and tore headlong down the hill with no thought of the direction in which they ran.

"I never want to see *that* place again," Jimmy was finally able to gasp. "I didn't know Injun's bones could turn so white. How long do you think that skeleton's been there?"

"A hundred years, anyway," was Frank's awed reply. "The canoe was rotten as punk."

"I wonder why it was sitting up like that?" Jimmy asked, shuddering a little at the memory.

"Some Injun custom maybe," Frank said, glancing over his shoulder nervously. "Let's keep moving."

The boys were greatly cheered presently by stumbling across the faint traces of a pathway, overgrown with salal bushes, but still a trail of sorts. But this, too, presented a problem; in one direction no doubt lay the village, in the other the far-reaching forest which, as far as they knew, had no end. Neither of them had the vaguest idea as to which direction they should take.

The rain had almost stopped, but a dense fog had crossed the strait from the Vancouver Island shore to settle like a gloomy pall among the dripping trees. Suddenly a booming sound echoed through the forest, a distant, deep-throated cry that was repeated at regular intervals.

"It's the steam fog horn on Tatoosh Island!" Frank exclaimed. "The fog's got so thick they've started up the whistle."

He stood a moment in deep thought, then in an excited voice continued, "I've got an idea. Leaving the bay, Tatoosh Island was on our right side. Going back it should be on the left. It's on our right side now, from the sound of the fog horn, so that shows we've been traveling away from home instead of toward it. If we keep the fog horn on our left side it will guide us to the bay."

The trail curved in a serpentine and wayward course through the timber, but the boys were happy to be assured by

80

the guiding blasts of the Tatoosh Island fog horn that it was continuing to lead them toward the village. Finally the overgrown trail joined up with a well defined wood road and from there on their progress was more rapid. Even so it was almost dark when the boys, footsore, wet, weary and carrying empty berry buckets, trudged into the village.

"I'll be a nervous wreck some day, worrying about you boys," their mother exclaimed when they presented themselves at the kitchen door, their faces scratched, their hair and clothing disheveled and their shoes squelching soggily in pools of dripping water. "I was just on the point of sending Lighthouse Jack out to hunt for you. I see you haven't any huckleberries, so there will be no pies tonight, but we won't bother about that now."

Alternating scolding and hugging her two wayward boys, Mrs. McCurdy supervised a change to warm, dry clothing and then joined her husband and Captain Zem, the proprietor of the village trading post, in listening to the boys 'wide-eyed account of their day's adventures.

Captain Zem, who had lived with the Makahs longer than any of the other whites, had a ready explanation of the peculiar posture of the dead Indian in the decayed canoe, and he told the story with all the relish of a born spinner of yarns:

"The Indians say that many years ago a member of the tribe died and was buried in his canoe, as was the custom at that time. But the supposed corpse revived, climbed out of the canoe and returned to the village dressed in his burial robes.

"His friends and relatives, believing he had entered into a league with evil spirits and having, besides, already divided his possessions among themselves, fell upon him with clubs and made sure he was really dead before they were finished with him. This incident annoyed them very much and, to prevent such a thing happening again, they began to bind the bodies of the dead with rawhide thongs.

"After that the tribe was never troubled by any supposed corpse coming back from his burial place. This custom, however, was given up long ago and the Indians now bury their dead in the ground like the whites, which is easier than lugging a big canoe into the woods to a proper *memaloose* place and burying the owner in it . . . and they also save the canoe, which is no small item."

Bewhiskered Captain Zem knocked out the ashes from his pipe on a corner of the fireplace and rose to take his departure. "And now to change the subject," he told the boys, "it looks to me that if it hadn't been for that fog horn out on Tatoosh you boys would have spent the night in the woods. I've heard of dozens of cases where sailors on the water have been helped by that horn, but you're about the only ones I know who got their bearings from it in the middle of the woods. Be sure and thank Keeper Samson when you see him."

The boys agreed that their heartfelt thanks were due the lighthouse keeper on the rocky offshore island and the opportunity of following Captain Zem's suggestion presented itself before many days had passed.

CHAPTER ELEVEN

At the Jumping Off Place

One of the duties of Jimmy's father was to keep the cluster of government buildings on Tatoosh Island in good condition. This giant rock, rising 150 feet above the restless Pacific, marks the most northwesterly point of the continental United States and is separated from the mainland at Cape Flattery by a half-mile of turbulent swells and breaking seas.

The island was selected as a lighthouse site by a joint Army and Navy commission which visited the Strait of Juan de Fuca in 1849, but the beacon was not completed and placed in operation until late in the year 1857.

Many of the Makahs had, in earlier years, spent the summer months there, occupying large cedar houses facing the beach and well above the high water mark and even though the island was now government property, tribesmen were often posted there to watch for whales and for changes in the weather.

While engaged in repair work at this isolated outpost in the sea, Mr. McCurdy had become well acquainted with Captain Alexander Samson, the head lighthouse keeper, who was thereafter welcomed at the hospitable McCurdy home whenever he visited Neah Bay.

Captain Samson was a big man, slightly stooped, with iron gray hair and beard and the weathered face of a man who has spent a lifetime at sea. His faded blue eyes under their slightly contracted lids seemed forever trying to focus their gaze upon some object on the far horizon. His voice was powerful and throaty, as though the great steam fog horn which had been his close companion for many years had imparted some of the deep-toned resonance of its voice to his own.

When Captain Samson next visited the village the boys took the opportunity to tell him how his fog whistle had helped them find their way home after their frightening experience in the forest. The recital greatly amused the old captain.

"I knew the Tatoosh horn was a blessing to sailors," he chuckled, "but this is the first time I've heard of it guiding a pair of landlubbers through the woods. I ought to report this to the Department so it can take credit for the performance."

The keeper clapped one big hand on Jimmy's shoulder and the other on Frank's. "By the way," he rumbled conspiratorially, "did you know the two of you are going to have a chance to see the big whistle at close range?"

The boys were too amazed and delighted to more than beam their approval as the captain continued:

"Well, you are, for your parents have decided to let you visit me on the island for a couple of weeks. I've got a lot of things to show you and plenty of interesting things to tell you about."

Sure enough, a few days later saw the two boys excited occupants of Lighthouse Jack's canoe, bound for Tatoosh Island seven miles to the westward beyond Cape Flattery and rising from the depths of the mighty Pacific Ocean itself.

Amiable Lighthouse Jack propelled his light craft with deft, steady strokes of the paddle, pointing out various objects of interest as they passed. Soon they left the relatively sheltered waters of Neah Bay and passed the ramlike bulwark of Koitlah Point which jutted like the prow of a great petrified battleship into the long swells of the strait. Beyond the point lay a treacherous reef stretching out like a skeleton arm as though trying to grip a similar arm extending from the Waadah Island shore opposite.

As the canoe rounded the point, Jack stopped paddling and remarked, "Very low tide today; perhaps we see old cannon."

Taking careful bearings on the shore and maneuvering his canoe skilfully into position against tide and current, he told the boys to look down into the clear salt water. Sure enough, lying on the bottom of firm sand some ten feet below the surface, they could make out the shape of an ancient muzzle-loading cannon, encrusted in barnacles and trailing graceful tendrils of seaweed.

"That cannon here many, many years," Jack explained. "Injuns tried to get it up, but too heavy for them."[8]

After this brief pause for a thrilling look through green sea water into a mysterious chapter of forgotten history, Jack sent the canoe knifing out into the Strait, the slim craft dancing over the long, lazy swells like a porpoise at play. After rounding another point, Tatoosh Island appeared wraithlike in the distant sea mist, like some sea monster resting upon the surface of the ocean. To the boys it seemed to represent the very rim of the world with nothing beyond but the boundless ocean.

The canoe skirted broad beds of kelp which formed minia-

---

[8]Some half a century later a diver who was working on a stranded steamer in the vicinity was shown this cannon by a very old Indian. With the aid of a scow and a couple of Indians, the diver succeeded in salvaging the cannon, which weighed about 350 pounds. Its identity has never been completely established, but it is believed to have belonged to the Hudson's Bay Company's trading vessel *Una*, wrecked on Koitlah Point in 1851.

ture Sargasso Seas along the shoreline, the citron-colored bulbs and streaming ribbons held in place by thick, rubbery stems attached firmly to the rocky bottom far below. Within the kelp beds numerous rocks broke the surface of the sea, gorgeously colored by clinging starfish of vivid hues, with purple, red and yellow predominating.

Just before Cape Flattery was reached, Jack detoured on a sightseeing voyage through hidden waterways among the rocks, just wide enough to permit passage of the canoe. At one point Jack paused and gestured to seaward like an artist displaying his prize work; through an arched rock Tatoosh Island lay like a three-dimensional picture framed in grotesque stone.

Then, with a quick twirl of his paddle, the Indian sent the canoe darting toward the open sea to breast the profound gray swells of the world's mightiest ocean. As the tiny craft swiftly crossed the mile of open sea separating the cape from the island, the grim bulk of Tatoosh seemed to lift itself from the Pacific and move forward to meet them.

As Lighthouse Jack sent the canoe skimming past the line of white breakers at the rock's base, the boys looked with awe at the mysterious caverns into which the seas rushed and rhythmically retreated. The whole rocky base of the island, they discovered, was honeycombed by the age-old action of the restless Pacific waves, but upon this foundation of tortured stone rests a deposit of rich soil supporting a heavy growth of emerald green grass. The contrast between the fearsome sea caves below and the orderly white buildings and the neat green lawns far above gave an air of unreality to their surroundings.

A fragment of the rock's northern end had apparently in past ages started to break away and slip into the ocean depths, but when about half submerged it had ceased to sink and had remained attached to the parent island by a ridge of stone. This act of nature had resulted in the formation of a small cove with a short stretch of sandy shore and it was here that Lighthouse Jack landed his canoe. Captain Samson, who had kept his long brass telescope trained on them as they crossed from the mainland, was on hand to conduct the boys to the high plateau above by means of a narrow path cut into the rocky cliff.

Spread out over the level expanse of the island's top was a sizeable group of buildings, all painted a dazzling white and each serving its particular purpose in the highly specialized functions of the Tatoosh Island Light Station. There was the weather station, securely anchored with iron chains attached to deeply embedded rods, for the tremendous winter storms of the North Pacific sometimes send seas crashing clear across the island's lofty top and, a few years earlier, a great wind of hurricane force had torn the roof from the lighthouse itself. Similarly well anchored and constructed of heavy masonry were the display and signal offices, fog signal house and keepers' dwellings. Dwarfing all these lesser structures was the light tower of brick masonry rising 65 feet above the central keeper's dwelling of sturdy sandstone.

Of course the first thing anyone wants to do when visiting a lighthouse is to climb to the top of the tower and Frank and Jimmy were no exception to the rule. They climbed the spiraling iron stairway to the watch room, a small compartment immediately under the light. Captain Samson pointed out the coal oil tanks which fed the powerful beacon above.

"Regulations say coal oil's supposed t'do the trick," he told the boys, "but I've learned a few tricks about tendin' a light in the years I've been here. The inspectors don't know it, but I always add a dash of whale oil and lard t'make it gleam a little brighter."

The captain beckoned to the boys and they followed him to the topmost iron step of the tower, where the old keeper paused to pull back a heavy storm door and they entered the circular, glass-walled lantern room. The boys gasped at the beauty of the jewel-like beacon which, though unlighted, glittered brilliantly behind its intricate glass lens.

The boys didn't have to be told by Captain Samson that this was the heart and soul of the lighthouse, or that it was a thing to be viewed from a distance and not touched. The lives of countless men had been saved by its warning beam and the lives of other men had been sacrificed to place it there and to keep it burning bright from dusk to dawn. They circled it, pausing to read the brass plate riveted to its base:

Fresnel light, 1st order, constructed by order of Hon. the Secretary of the Treasury of the United States and the Lighthouse Board, W. A. Bartlett, Lieut. U. S. Navy special superintendent. Louis Sautter & Co., constructors, Paris 1854.[9]

"What is that red strip of glass set in the lens for?" Jimmy asked Captain Samson after his inspection was completed.

"That throws a red ray out over Duncan Rock," the keeper explained. "Duncan Rock lies about a mile off the island and just awash, ready to rip the bottom out of the stoutest ship ever built. When seamen get close to that red ray at night they keep a mighty good watch until they're well through it."

He led the boys to the iron-railed catwalk which encircled the great glass lantern, pointing to where the insweeping rollers of the Pacific broke in a white welter about the barely concealed fangs of Duncan Rock. Below them spread the green surface of Tatoosh, dotted with the red roofs of neat white buildings. To the east lay the primeval rain forest of the Washington coast behind the frowning rampart of Cape Flattery. To the west lay

---

[9]The same lens and fittings are still in use at the station (1960), although electricity has replaced kerosene as the lamp's fuel.

only the solemnly marching waves of the Pacific, diminishing and fading into a hazy, unmarked horizon.

The boys leaned spellbound against the iron railing in this enchanted place between sky and sea, watching a coastwise passenger steamship crawl toward them from the south, its sidewheels clawing at the gray water and a flaunting banner of coal smoke streaking from its tall, raked funnel. When it came close and changed course to enter the Strait of Juan de Fuca they could see passengers on the upper deck, below the ponderously nodding walking-beam, staring at the desolate little island and its guardian beacon.

"It's the *Dakota,* from San Francisco," Captain Samson's deep voice boomed out behind them to break their reverie. "The steward's 'll be ringin' the gongs for lunch aboard her about now, so let's take the hint an' see what the cook's got ready for us down below."

After a hearty lunch the boys explored the limited confines of the island. At its westernmost tip they were surprised to see a white signboard nailed to a fence post. Pointed at both ends, it bore two neatly painted hands, one pointing east, the other west. The western marker bore the legend, "China: 6000 miles;" the one pointing east was lettered, "United States: 1 mile." This, Captain Samson explained, was the work of an assistant keeper who, beside being somewhat of a humorist, aspired to be a poet. He had embellished the otherwise dry pages of the lighthouse logbook with a number of his verses, some of which Jimmy considered far superior to the selections in his school reader. He made it a point to memorize several of the shorter ones through which ships, sailors and beacons passed in stately procession. One, entitled *Cape Flattery Light,* closed with this stirring verse:

> "And on dark, stormy nights when far at sea,
>   This beacon bursts upon the mariners' sight;
>   They shape their course, from doubt and danger free,
>   And bless the keepers of Cape Flattery Light."

This poem, though long and full of difficult words, Jimmy considered so splendid that he memorized it in its entirety, planning to add new laurels to his fame as a "reciter" when he returned to school in the fall.

In the evening, snug beside the big stove in the keepers' quarters below the sweeping ray of the light, the boys listened to Captain Samson spin yarns of Tatoosh Island and the treacherous seas around it. They learned that the builders of the lighthouse had been forced to defend themselves in pitched battles against the Makahs, who had been completely savage in those days and who considered Tatoosh to be their private tribal whaling station and summer resort.

He told them that the 8000-candlepower lamp, which now burned kerosene, had formerly used lard oil, but that occasionally, when regular fuel ran short, whale oil had been bought from the Indians for emergency use. It is the one inviolate rule of the Lighthouse Service that the beacon must be kept burning at any cost and, on this desolate frontier coastline a lighthouse keeper had need of considerable ingenuity to keep that rule intact.

While the sea wind moaned outside and the fire crackled cozily in the stove the old keeper explained that, although the tower was built of solid brick and dovetailed stone, it had been known to shudder and sway violently when the full force of the winter storms were unleashed against the great shaft. Men new at the work had been known to desert the lofty lantern room at such times, believing the tower was about to collapse. Although the light's focal plane was 200 feet above the sea, the salt spray from the crashing waves would sweep across the glass lantern room during those terrible storms and the keepers would have to spend uncomfortable hours on the outside catwalk polishing the lens. Nothing must be allowed to dim that dazzling band of light that carried its warning to mariners twenty miles at sea.

During these heavy storms, the captain said, the keepers had literally to crawl upon their hands and knees to avoid being swept off the island by sudden gusts which had been measured at a hundred miles an hour and more. In the morning after such severe storms, scores of dead sea birds would be found encircling the base of the tower. Attracted by the light, they would come driving through the darkness of the night to crash against the lens with tremendous force.

The huge, trumpet-shaped foghorn which had the distinction of occupying its own separate house, within which was the steam boiler, water tank and bright red whistle engine, had a special fascination for the boys and they were anxious to hear it in operation at close range. They were soon to have this wish gratified, for early on the second evening of their stay on the island a dense fog bank came rolling ominously in from the westward, enveloping the island and then the coastline in a ghostly shroud.

Jimmy and Frank, who had been in the watch room high in the lighthouse, had watched the lights of a distant steamship soften and go out with gentle abruptness as the advancing fog enveloped them. Then they raced down the iron stairway in search of Captain Samson, who had been expecting them.

"They'll be starting the whistle any minute now," he told them. "Do you want to go down and see how it's done?"

He was talking to an empty room. The boys were already headed at full speed toward the fog horn building. Inside they saw that steam was high in the boiler and an assistant keeper was at the red engine. He had opened the drains and the exhaust and had his hand on the throttle, waiting the inevitable order.

Captain Samson entered the building, puffing a bit from trying to keep up with his eager young guests. The first tendrils of fog were already drifting by outside and he wasted no time in giving the order.

"Start the whistle."

The assistant keeper opened the valve slowly, the heavy fly-wheel revolved and the small building shuddered with the awful roar of the great whistle which thrust its trumpet-head through the masonry wall toward the invisible sea. To the boys, standing directly behind it, the monstrous voice of the fog horn was a frightening thing. It seemed impossible that human ear-drums could withstand the force of such sound.

When the keeper signified, between horn blasts, that he was ready to return to the main building, Jimmy and Frank were happy enough to follow him. From inside the thick-walled house the deeply resonant tones of the horn booming out over the sullen waters were pleasantly muted and Jimmy thought it would be a fine evening for Captain Samson to spin yarns of fog and shipwreck.

CHAPTER TWELVE

Tales of Tatoosh

The great fog bank had enfolded Tatoosh Island completely. The stars had disappeared and the dark loom of the North American continent to the east. It seemed to Jimmy and his brother that the world had shrunk to their tiny island with its great light shrouded in the mist and its steam trumpet crying into the darkness.

Captain Samson drew his armchair close to the stove and carefully filled his stubby pipe with black tobacco, which he shaved precisely from a great plug he carried in his hip pocket wrapped in oilskin.

"Fog," the old keeper said, when he had the odorous pipe going to his satisfaction, "is about the worst thing a sailor man has to contend with, especially when he's trying to make a proper landfall off this coast. Many's the stout ship and good crew that's ended up on the Graveyard on just such a night as this."

"The Graveyard, sir?" prompted Jimmy, wide-eyed. Captain Samson's yarn-spinning was taking just the course he had hoped it would and he was careful not to break the old man's train of thought.

Captain Samson gestured with his pipe toward the black void to the north. "Vancouver Island," he explained. "Sailors call that wall of rock across there the Graveyard, and with good reason."

The captain rose from his chair and moved to a framed chart bolted to the wall. "Y'see," he continued, "a ship headed up the coast or in from across the Pacific and bound for Puget Sound has to make her landfall off the island here," he pointed to the tiny dot that represented Tatoosh, "and she has to sail in straight and true between here and the Graveyard over there." His stubby finger indicated the long line of the Vancouver Island coast to the north.

Jimmy inspected the chart, comparing the scale of nautical miles on the lower corner to the white gap of fathom-marked water separating the coast of Washington Territory from the Canadian island to the north.

"But the Strait must be pretty near twelve miles wide between here and Van— and the Graveyard," he said. "Seems like a captain who knows his business could hit a channel twelve miles wide even with his eyes shut."

Captain Samson shook his head. "T'aint quite that simple," he explained patiently. His broad hand swept up the line of Washington coast pictured on the chart. "Y'see, the Kura Shima, the black current from Japan, sweeps north up the coast here, like a giant river flowing in the ocean, and it slams up against the Vancouver Island coast with the power o' ten thousand miles behind it. Combine that with the tides and the eddies and the fact that the wind seems to be able to blow from two directions at once out here and the master of a sailin' ship's likely to have trouble on his hands when the sun's shinin' and everything's shipshape. And heaven help him on a night like this."

Jimmy was still studying the chart. He pointed to the almost invisible gap of white which separated Tatoosh Island from the ram's-head of Cape Flattery, the narrow channel which he and Frank had crossed in Lighthouse Jack's canoe.

"Do big ships ever use this way to get into the Strait?" he asked.

Captain Samson returned to his chair to puff reflectively on his pipe. "One did once," he said, "and it was a sight I won't forget to my dyin' day."

Jimmy and Frank returned to their seats as quietly as they could. The captain, they felt, was about to embark on a tale which would do proper credit to this night of coldly drifting fog and to the accompaniment of the great steam trumpet.

"The channel that separates Tatoosh from the Cape is full of reefs and hidden rocks, as you boys have seen for yourselves," he began. "The only deep water lies right under the island and only Indian canoes and a few little fishing boats ever try to go that way."

The captain knocked the ashes from his pipe into his horny hand and deposited them neatly in the stove before continuing.

"Well, one fall we'd been having a spell of dense fog that was the worst I'd ever seen and the horn had been going day and night for weeks on end. The lighthouse tender hadn't been able to get out and we were a month overdue for supplies and mail. We hadn't even seen the mainland for weeks and there was nothing to do but sit around and hate each other and listen for that horn to beller every two minutes.

"One afternoon somebody yelled that the fog was clearing away a little and we all rushed outside for a look around. In a minute somebody else let out a shout that *was* a shout and there, almost close enough to harpoon, was a great three-masted square-rigger booming through that channel with every sail set.

"I could see the officers on her quarterdeck as clear as I can see you and it was easy to tell they were as surprised as we were to see the lighthouse looming over heir heads and those rock fangs grinnin' up at 'em from every side.

"I grabbed my speaking trumpet and made a dash to the edge of the island, shouting directions and motioning for them to draw her over as close as possible to the island. I saw the captain nod his head and I could see the scared whites of the helmsman's eyes as he swung the wheel spokes. Then the great, slim hull was driving past right under my feet and I'll swear I could feel the wind of her sails as she rushed past.

"They cleared the channel as by a miracle, dipped their flag, mind you, by way of saying thanks, and then disappeared as quick as they'd come in the fog that closed in as thick as ever and stayed that way for another solid week or more. We never did learn the name of that big square-rigger, but she had good reason to remember us."

As the evening wore on the captain told the boys other tales and legends of lonely Tatoosh; how, on another foggy night years before a group of thirteen strange men appeared at the keeper's door, wet, hungry and almost exhausted. They had constituted the crew of the American ship *Persevere*, which had been making a voyage from San Francisco to Victoria for a cargo of coal. She ran into a heavy gale some forty miles off Cape Flattery and, being old and rotten, soon began to go to pieces. The crew took to the boats, leaving everything behind them, which was a wise move, for they had hardly gone over the rail when the ship rolled over and went down like a rock.

To make matters worse, a fog bank was drifting in from the west on the heels of the storm, requiring the sailors to throw all their strength into a race through still violent seas to reach the distant beacon of Tatoosh before it was blotted out by the fog.

After pulling for many hours they finally reached the island with barely enough strength left to crawl up the narrow rock path from beach to lighthouse. They were given hot food and warm clothing by the keepers and, after a sojourn of several weeks on the island, they were taken off by the lighthouse tender and safely landed at Portland.

Soon Captain Samson noticed that his young friends were growing heavy-eyed and Jimmy, despite his best efforts to remain alert, was nodding in his chair.

"Avast there," the old keeper roared in his best fog horn voice. "It's into your bunks with you. You'll find the old horn the finest lullaby that ever sang a boy to sleep."

The boys stumbled sleepily to their room and found the captain's prediction entirely accurate. From under the blankets

Jimmy counted three solemnly measured blasts from the horn. After that he remembered nothing until he awoke to see a bright beam of sunlight slanting through the room's narrow window.

The fine weather continued and the boys proceeded to explore every inch of the island's seventeen-acre surface. On one placid day, with the tide low and the seas gentle, Captain Samson even conducted them through the two awesome caves that passed completely through the island's base and through which the ocean surges roared and bellowed during the winter storms.

"When the whole North Pacific seems to be trying to get through here all at once it causes considerable commotion," the captain said. "It sounds like a combination of all the thunder-claps in the world and it makes you feel as if it's going to force the island up in the air. It's a good thing there's some air holes to relieve some of the pressure or I do believe it would lift the top of the island off its foundations like the lid off a tea kettle."

When they emerged at the island's southern base Jimmy pointed across the narrow channel which separated Tatoosh from the mainland to where, a mile south of the Cape, a great pinnacle of rock towered above the breaking surf.

"It looks like a big face looking out over the sea," Jimmy commented.

"I've often had the same fancy," the captain said. "It's known as Fuca's Pillar[10] and it's over a hundred feet high. It looks like this spell of good weather's due to hold on a while, so I'll talk to Lighthouse Jack when he brings the mail out from Neah Bay this afternoon and maybe he'll take you over to see it. He'll probably tell you an Indian legend or two about it along the way."

Lighthouse Jack was his usual amiable self and he had no objection to conducting the boys on a tour of the coastline. As a matter of fact, Jack seemed to take a personal pride in the wild grandeur of his homeland and enjoyed nothing more than pointing out its wonders to a properly appreciative audience.

As the Indian mail carrier drove his canoe diagonally across the channel toward Fuca's Pillar the boys realized for the first time what an immense and massive column of stone it was and, as Captain Samson had intimated, Lighthouse Jack had a great legend to tell about it.

In the *ahncutty* days . . . long, long ago, Jack told them, the young braves of the Makah tribe used this rock to test their

---

[10]The Greek pilot, Juan de Fuca, claimed to have discovered the entrance to a great inland sea between 48 and 49 degrees latitude during a voyage in the service of the Viceroy of Mexico in 1592. Many historians claim Fuca's claims were purely imaginary, but his writings include a remarkably accurate description of Cape Flattery and Fuca's Pillar:

"And at the entrance of the said strait there is on the North West coast thereof a great Headland or Island, with an exceeding high Pinnacle of spired rock like a pillar thereupon." Jas. G. McCurdy believed that Juan de Fuca's story was true.

personal prowess, each trying to outdo the others in climbing the perpendicular sides of the great pillar, which they called *Tea-Tea-Dak*. Each one who gained a loftier foothold than any who had gone before him marked the place with the totem of his family, thus gaining great prestige for himself and his entire clan.

At last a sure-footed young Indian of adventurous spirit and great courage succeeded in reaching a higher spot than had ever been attained before; but not satisfied with this and led on by ambition and pride, he kept on climbing high above any other mark and there carved the two-headed bear, the symbol of his house.

This was a great triumph for the young brave, but his muscles had been badly overtaxed and he found that they could no longer be depended upon to respond properly to his will. As he endeavored to climb down from his lofty perch, he narrowly escaped losing his footing and being dashed to pieces on the rocks far below, where the voices of his companions sounded like a distant murmur of waters. Again and again he tried desperately to work his way downward, but it seemed that the *seatcos*, the dark spirits of the rock, were angry at his boldness and proposed to hold him prisoner.

For he found that he could still climb upward and this, at last, he did, following an upward slanting fissure and reaching from toe-hold to jagged toe-hold until at length, utterly exhausted, he sprawled out upon a small, grass-covered area at the very summit.

His friends did their best to rescue him from this precarious refuge. The strongest bowmen tried to shoot a line over the rock, but the distance was too great. They tied light lines to the legs of ducks and sea gulls and tried to make them fly over the rock, but the birds, thus hampered and frightened, refused to rise. At last, convinced that it was the desire of the spirits that their friend be left as a sacrifice, the other Indians returned to the village, leaving the young brave to meet a lingering death by thirst and starvation on the summit of the great rock in the sea.

Probably his bones still rested there, for according to Lighthouse Jack, the rock was considered a *cultus* place after that tragedy and the young braves no longer climbed its steep sides. But the Makahs believe, too, that the spirit of the brave young warrior still guards the rock and gives warning, by means known only to the wisest of the medicine men, of approaching storms. They give thought, when passing Fuca's Pillar, to the youth whose ambition led him to a lingering death.

Leaving this ill-omened place, Jack sent the canoe along the surf line toward the Cape Flattery sea caves, some of which extended far into the interior of the rocky cliffs. As they approached the caves the towering bluff above them sloped outward, reflecting the rays of the afternoon sun and leaving the waters at their feet in glimmering semi-darkness. Thousands of sea parrots, gulls and ducks, disturbed in their nesting places upon the projecting cornices of rock, flew about the canoe with raucous cries and a wild beating of wings. The long, lazy ocean swells dashed against the abrupt ramparts of the Cape with a muffled booming sound and were lost in the deep mysteries of the sea caves.

Jack carefully maneuvered his canoe in the uncertain light, allowing the boys to peer into the mouths of the dark caverns, which he made no attempt to enter.

In the old days, when seals were plentiful in these waters, he told his passengers, some of the best harpooners would station themselves on rocks just inside the caves while other hunters went out to sea in the whaling canoes to drive the herds of seal and sea otter toward the cliffs. When the frightened mammals sought refuge in the caves the waiting hunters would spear them. The women would have driftwood fires prepared on a nearby beach, where the bodies of the slain animals would be dragged for skinning and the boiling out of the oil.

Many years ago while the Makahs were thus peacefully engaged at the caves, a swarm of piratical savages from the Queen Charlotte Islands suddenly swept in from the sea in their huge war canoes and fell upon the unarmed fishermen. They killed a number of the Makahs, who tried to defend themselves with rocks and fishing spears, and the remainder were forced to take shelter in the caves where their superstitious enemies dared not follow them.

The plight of those marooned in the gloomy caverns was desperate. A few trickles of fresh water seeped through cracks in the cave roof and they found a few morsels of shellfish, which they ate raw, but they knew they could not survive there for long.

Several canoes that sought to escape by stealing out at night were promptly detected by the vigilant foe and their crews were put to a speedy death. Finally a stalwart young brave volunteered to make a desperate try to reach Neah Bay and summon help.

Creeping to the cave entrance through surging seas, he swung himself upward at the entrance and began climbing the face of the overhanging cliff. The Northern Indians, intent on preventing escape by sea, did not discover the agile climber in the darkness above their heads and, having reached the top, he made his way through tangled underbrush and across deep canyons where no trails existed.

After covering seven terrible miles through the dark forest he arrived at the village in the early morning, covered with cuts and bruises and almost fainting from exhaustion and loss of blood. But he still had sufficient strength to report the plight of the fisherman besieged in the sea caves of Flattery.

Within a few hours a flotilla of Makah canoes filled with armed warriors carrying spears, bows and heavy, cannonball-shaped stones dashed around the tip of Cape Flattery. With loud war cries the relief party fell upon the surprised Northern savages, while the besieged hunters swarmed out of the caves to reinforce their brethren and revenge themselves upon their enemies.

For several hours the battle raged, with neither side able to gain a decisive advantage. After a period of long distance fighting, in which the Makahs held their own, the conflict became a hand to hand one. The Makahs were expert in hurling their great stone cannonballs, which they used to crack the heads of their enemies as well as to crush the sides of their war canoes.

The northerners were willing to face the terrible hail of stones, but the destruction of their canoes apalled them. If it continued it would leave them stranded on a hostile shore many miles from home. At a shouted word of command from their leader, they abandoned the fight and, picking up their wounded, were soon in full retreat, spurred on by showers of arrows and flung spears from the outraged Makahs. Many years passed before the warlike savages from the north dared to again attack the Makahs.

Jimmy and his brother were glad to learn of the successful end of this sea battle which, had it not been for the valor of one Indian, might have ended tragically for their Makah friends. The sun was now low on the sea behind the black outline of Tatoosh Island and they were glad, too, when Lighthouse Jack turned the canoe's prow for the return voyage to the light station. Salt air and tales of adventure have a whetting effect on youthful appetites. Supper would soon be served in the galley at the keepers' house and they wanted to be on hand when it was.

On their return to the island the boys saw a curious sight which they had not noticed before. Lodged in a deep crevice of a great rock, high above the reach of the mightiest waves, was a long, bleached log, one splintered end pointing out to sea.

Lighthouse Jack explained its presence simply. "When the man who made the world finish his work, he have this one big piece of timber left. So he put it here where nobody can reach it and it be safe. Its been there as long as Makahs remember, but some day Great Spirit come to get it when he have more building to do."

That night, their last on the island, Jimmy and Frank discussed the legends of Lighthouse Jack.

"His stories are fun to listen to," Frank said with a touch of scorn in his voice, "but only a baby would believe them. They don't make sense."

Jimmy lay in his bunk, staring thoughtfully into the darkness of their snug room below the lighthouse. "I don't know," he said thoughtfully. "Some of them sound like sort of miracles, but so does Cap'n Samson's story about the ship under the island and the fog that lifted just long enough to save the lives of her crew . . . and you believe *him,* don't you?"

There was no answer from the other bunk. Frank was asleep.

Jimmy lay awake for a long time, thinking of the things he had learned at Tatoosh Island and in the canoe of Lighthouse Jack. He remembered something a traveling preacher had said during services in the schoolhouse at Neah Bay . . . something about men who go down to the sea in ships and see the wonders of the Lord on deep waters.

He decided, before he too drifted into slumber, that men in lighthouses on rocky islands in the sea have a mighty fine chance to learn about such things, too.

CHAPTER THIRTEEN

Captain Zem

Next to the Agent himself, Captain Zemro Cutler was regarded as the most important personage on the Reservation, to which Frank and Jimmy had returned after their stay on Tatoosh Island. Certainly he was viewed as a man of great importance by all the boys of the village, who considered his trading post as the center of their restricted universe.

Captain Zem, as he liked to be called, had roamed about the Northwest country for many years as miner, mariner and trader, but he had settled down at Neah Bay at least thirty years ago, having been granted a licensed trader's commission by the Indian Department. He had never married, but he was vastly fond of children, who ran to him with all their questions and problems. The whiskery old fellow was particularly adept at answering questions about the Neah Bay country, for he had made a long study of its early history as well as its Indian legends and was considered an authority even by the adults of the community.

The store which he operated for the accommodation of whites and Indians alike was one of the showplaces of the village, although to most visitors the sagging frame building was uninspiring on the outside and almost unbelievably cluttered on the inside. Captain Zem prided himself on the fact that his establishment stocked everything "from a needle to an anchor." Groceries were piled helter-skelter at the back of the room. Indian baskets, mats, miniature canoes, totems and other souvenirs for the tourist trade mingled with clothing, blankets and piece goods upon the shelves or under them. Show cases were jammed full of gaudy notions calculated to attract the eyes of Indian customers.

Colored beads by the keg, molasses and raw sugar by the barrel, flour in sacks, hard-tack in boxes and kerosene in cans littered the floor, while rancid butter, plug tobacco of the kind favored by Captain Samson, stale candy and strong cheese lay in a confused mass upon the counters. Strangely enough, Captain Zem and his two Indian clerks could instantly place their fingers upon any item of this tangled stock.

A fish stall occupied one corner of the store and a ten by twelve-foot lean-to at the rear housed the Neah Bay postoffice, Captain Zem officiating as postmaster. Odors of many varieties, with that of fish predominating, filled every cranny not otherwise occupied, but this mixture of exotic and domestic smells was an important factor in the charm of Captain Zem's store had for the younger generation of the village.

The old trader added to his income by purchasing seal skins from the Indians, which he cured and salted for shipment to England, but his efforts to build up a fresh fish business with outside connections had ended in failure. Neah Bay was too remote from the markets of the growing towns on Puget Sound and dependable transportation facilities were not available.

The beach in front of Captain Zem's store was an animated, colorful place during business hours, with dozens of canoes flitting about the bay or drawn up, side by side, just above high water mark. The Indians always came and went with the tide, no matter how long a journey might be delayed. A favorable tide meant easy going, while bucking a head tide meant continuous muscular exertion. Besides, no Indian would subject his beloved canoe to the wear and tear of being dragged over a gravelly beach at low tide.

Standing out from all the other craft on this crowded waterfront was the "Washington Canoe," a huge craft over sixty feet in length, hewn from the trunk of a single Western red cedar tree. This mighty craft was the property of the Indian Department and had been used for years by Indian Agents when visiting the more remote parts of the reservation. Now it was beginning to show decay above the waterline and was no longer considered seaworthy. The rains had partially filled it with water, and the boys of the village had taken to using it as a swimming pool during the warm summer days.

On this account they viewed with deep disapproval a project by Young Doctor and some of his helpers to make repairs on the big canoe. They openly expressed the opinion that the ancient craft could never be made seaworthy, but their comments were ignored and no one answered their questions as to why the repairs were being made.

They did not have to wait long to solve the mystery, however, for early one morning the old craft was launched by a group of Indians and loaded with a great assortment of vegetables from the reservation farm, under the direction of Lenwood Fisher, the government farmer. The plan, they learned, was to tow the loaded canoe to Bahada and turn the cargo over to the cook at the Indian boarding school.

Six canoes were made fast to the monster craft and the order was given to begin the voyage across the bay. As the flotilla pulled out it was beset by a rising wind and heavy swells and towing the deeply laden craft proved a slow and laborious task. By the time half the distance had been covered a sudden black squall had come tearing in from the ocean.

The bay was soon a smother of foam-crested breakers and, to save themselves and their own canoes from injury, the Indians cut the laboring craft adrift. It was then a matter of only a short time before the ancient canoe, with a great crash, struck the beach broadside and was reduced to a mass of kindling wood.

Vegetables were strewn from one end of the bay to the other as an aftermath to the dramatic end of the Washington Canoe's long career. As for Captain Zem, he bribed the boys with penny candy to comb the beach and bring the salvaged vegetables to him, where they were placed on sale, at reduced prices, among the trader's other weird miscellany of tangled stock.

At the western edge of the village was another government craft of an entirely different type from the ancient canoe. This was a modern self-bailing, self-righting lifeboat which was carefully housed in the lifesaving station which Jimmy's father had built especially for it. The handsome lifeboat rested on its wheeled cradle, ready to be quickly launched in time of need. A pair of rails ran down to deep water from the front of the building for this purpose.

Fred Matheson who, with his family, occupied the second story of the lifesaving station, had charge of the boat, its gear and the building in general, keeping everything in spotless condition. While the boys were always welcome at the Matheson's, they were never allowed upon the holy-stoned lower floor, where the lifeboat rested in state, except in their bare feet.

About twice a year there was great excitement at the lifesaving station when a revenue cutter would anchor in the bay and a party of goldbraided officials would be rowed ashore to inspect the installation. When this occurred, the boys would desert the trading post and even Captain Zem would leave the store in charge of an Indian clerk and go puffing up the beach to watch the goings-on.

During the course of the inspection the lifeboat would be launched by a crew from the cutter and put through various maneuvers. Then the lifesaving gun would be tested, a cross-arm representing a shipwrecked vessel being planted in the sand at a distance and a shell fired in its direction with the life-line attached. More often than not the shot would go wild or drop short of the target, but eventually the line would be dropped over the cross-arm and a sailor would come sliding down in the breeches-buoy, usually looking rather disgusted at the long time it had taken to "rescue" him.

All this fuss was of little practical use, for Mr. Matheson

had no regular boat crew assigned him and was supposed to gather volunteers from among the Indian boatmen should an emergency arise. But the maneuvers gave great pleasure to the crowd of boys, white and red, who stood around open-mouthed, getting under the feet of sweating revenue cutter men and having a wonderful time in general. The labor involved in these periodic inspections was well justified in the eyes of Jimmy and his friends.[11]

On a slight sandy elevation near the mouth of the creek and overlooking the harbor was the site of an old Spanish fort. The boys had heard various stories about this ancient stronghold and, as usual, had asked Captain Zem to tell them all about it.

"Well, of course I never saw the fort," Captain Zem admitted, "but I've talked to the oldest Indians who were here when I came and some of them had seen it when they were youngsters. Then I've read considerable about it, so putting two and two together, I've a pretty good idea why it was built and how it looked.

"In the spring of 1792, Lieutenant Fidalgo was sent over here from Nootka, on the west coast of Vancouver Island where the Spanish had a settlement, to fortify this bay and keep the ships of other nations out of the Strait if he could. A small fort, mounting six guns, was built of logs and surrounded with a stockade. A bakery with oven and chimney of peculiar flat bricks from Mexico or Spain was built and those bakery bricks are about all that's left of the old Spanish fort.

"The Makahs didn't like the idea of a fort in their front yard and on their own ground, so there was constant bad blood between them and the Spaniards. A man from the fort named Serantes was waylaid while hunting and brutally murdered. When the Indians refused to give up the murderers, Fidalgo opened fire with the cannon on the village and killed a number of the Indians.

"The English and Spaniards had been quarreling for a long time at Nootka over ownership of the country. Finally the two nations went to war over that and other things. Spain, as usual, got the worst of it and had to give up her possessions along this coast. That fall Fidalgo had the fort torn down and

---

11Some years later, in February,1884, the lifeboat, manned by a volunteer Indian crew, put forth to the assistance of the 434-ton American bark *Lizzie Marshall*, wrecked on the bleak Vancouver Island coast at Bonilla Point, almost opposite Neah Bay across the Strait of Juan de Fuca. The vessel lay wedged among the rocks, having been caught in a dense fog and a flat calm that gave her no steerage way. The sight of the wreck was too much for the easy discipline of the Makah boat crew, descendents of generations of Indian pirates, and they swarmed aboard the bark intent upon loot. The lifeboat, left insecurely moored, broke away and drifted upon the rocks, smashing a great hole in her hull. The erstwhile rescuers, together with the ship's crew, remained marooned on the wreck, which soon began to break up in a heavy southwest gale. The stern section broke loose and was jammed between the rocks inside the reef, forming a bridge over which all hands reached the rocks and from them leaped to shore. Such was the ignominious end of the gallant Neah Bay lifeboat, of which Keeper Matheson had been so proud.

took everything of value in his ship back to Nootka, but to this day the Makahs say their fathers drove the Spaniards away and burned down the fort."

Such was the romantic history of the old Spanish fort at Neah Bay, but business was always uppermost in the mind of Captain Zem and he ended even this tale with a business-like suggestion.

"Now I'll tell you about those flat, yellow bricks from the fort's bakery," he said. "They're about eight inches long and five inches wide and an inch thick. A good many of them have been found and there's some up at the Territorial University in Seattle. I sell them to tourists and I'll give you two bits cash for any you find, but you won't find many. The best time to look is when the creek changes its course, which happens every so often."

Entranced by visions of sudden wealth, Jimmy and his brothers kept canny eyes peeled on the creek and, not long after their conversation with the old trader, they discovered that a heavy rainfall had caused the stream to leap its banks and make a new channel. They wasted no time in digging into the bed of the shallow creek. They unearthed six of the yellow bricks which they promptly sold to Captain Zem, convinced that they were well on the way to making their fortunes.

But though they dug like beavers, these were the only ones they ever found and they were convinced at last that the sole remaining vestiges of Neah Bay's ancient Spanish fort now reposed amid the fascinating clutter of Captain Zem's primitive department store.

CHAPTER FOURTEEN

In Pursuit of the Whale

Lighthouse Jack's reputation for dependability had been greatly enhanced by the fact that for years he had served the government as a seagoing postman, covering the mail route between Neah Bay and Tatoosh Island on a twice a week schedule which was almost as fixed as the tides.

Summer and winter, in fair weather and foul, his faithful canoe sped back and forth over the seven miles of treacherous Strait and ocean waters and seldom indeed had he failed to deliver his mail pouch.

During the winter season of awe-inspiring North Pacific storms it was often impossible for him to land on the narrow strip of beach at Tatoosh because of the crashing surf which would engulf the sloping sand to spout high against the island's craggy sides. On such occasions the courageous carrier of the government mail would make his canoe fast to an outlying kelp bed and wait for a propitious moment, gauging the in-sweeping seas with the practised eye of a born seaman.

Sensing a proper momentary balance of wind and wave, he would dart in toward the maelstrom at the island's base, throw the mail sack deftly to the keeper crouching on a rock to receive it and then fight his way back out to sea against the incoming surges. Although several canoes had been badly damaged in these breath-taking maneuvers, Jack had never failed to safely deliver the mail.

Lighthouse Jack was also regarded as one of the most thrifty of the reservation Indians. His dwelling, though built of the customary hand-hewn cedar planks, boasted a shake roof without the usual hole for the escape of smoke, for he was one of the few members of the tribe who possessed a stove. The neat brick chimney which crowned his dwelling was an undeniable mark of respectability and a constant source of pride to the Indian mail carier. His prized stove, in which his wife, Quedessa, shared the prestige of ownership, was long ago considered to have outlived its usefulness and had been condemned at the Government Building. Jack, seeing in it years of possible service, had swapped fish for it and almost swamped his canoe getting it home.

A small garden, lovingly tended by Quedessa, and the fresh seafood brought home by Jack provided the staples of their larder, but the proceeds of Jack's government mail check guaranteed an additional supply of sugar, tea, molasses and other *Boston muck-a-muck* (white man's food) from Captain Zem's store. By Makah standards, Lighthouse Jack and Quedesas led lives of true luxury.

Jimmy never tired of accompanying Jack on his fishing trips, during which the catch was likely to include such varied items as salmon, halibut, cod, huge Dungeness crabs, clams, limpets, sea-eggs, mussels and an occasional many-tentacled octopus, considered a great delicacy by the Indians, who made all their seafood dishes more tempting by liberal applications of whale and seal oil.

The finest varieties of shell fish could be found in great profusion on the rocky ledges of Waadah Island at low tide; and here one bright July morning Lighthouse Jack and Jimmy could have been found busily filling their baskets from the abundant supply nature had provided.

They were working on the far side of the island and consequently failed to observe a great commotion out in the Strait, several miles off the tip of Koitla Point. But a keen-eyed boy on the village waterfront had noticed the geyser-like plume of foamy spray shooting high in the air and the lazy antics of a huge black whale rolling in the broad waterway between the American and Canadian shores.

Instantly the magic word "Whale! Whale!" had gone echoing up and down the beach and, almost as quickly, a flotilla of ten big canoes was speeding seaward. Each canoe was manned by a crew of eight . . . six paddlers, a helmsman and *a* harpooner . . . and was equipped with harpoons, lances, ropes and sealskin floats.

With crews paddling like mad, away sped the canoes in the direction of the whale, each hoping to plant the first harpoon, an accomplishment which would insure both glory and a choice of the finest cuts of meat from the monster carcass when and if it was brought safely to land.

The medley of sounds soon reached the sharp ears of Lighthouse Jack and as he hastily launched his canoe, urged Jimmy aboard and paddling swiftly around the obstructing point a scene was unfolded which caused his eyes to flash and his heart to pound furiously. Out in the deep water of the Strait the whale was continuing its spouting and cavorting in evident enjoyment. Speeding in its direction, with paddles flashing in the sunshine, went the racing line of canoes.

The lure of the chase, implanted in every fibre of his nature by an age-old line of seagoing ancestors, was not be denied.

Jack simply had to take part in that whale hunt and share in the division of the spoils. But what to do with his small companion in the meantime was the momentous problem to be solved . . . and solved quickly.

To maroon poor Jimmy on Waadah Island, perhaps to fall into the sea from the slippery rocks or be attacked by the vicious wild pigs which roamed the beach, was not be thought of by a sober and responsible government official like Jack. To put him safely ashore at the village would, on the other hand, mean such a loss of time that participation in the hunt would be impossible. There was but one course open; he must take Jimmy with him.

As a salve to his conscience, Jack reflected that they could have but little part in the hunt since he had brought implements only for digging clams, not for killing whales. Furthermore, with ten canoes manned by expert hunters close at hand, no possible harm could come to the small boy in his keeping.

"You like hunt whale?" he asked Jimmy hopefully.

"Sure!" exclaimed the boy, his excitement hardly less keen than that of the veteran canoe-man.

"Good!" grunted Jack, and away they sped diagonally across the bay, quickly falling in behind the broken line of hunting canoes making for the open Strait. There was not one in that motley company of whalers more elated than Jimmy. To take part in a real whale hunt . . . what an opportunity for a white boy, especially one who had once been so weak and sickly that his parents had feared he might never walk again. What a story he could tell his envious companions upon his return! And with mighty Lighthouse Jack wielding the paddle, he didn't feel the least twinge of fear.

Jimmy had often inspected the whaling gear of the Makahs, which they kept always on hand for instant use should an occasion like this occur. The harpoon, the most important of the whale-catching weapons, had a head fashioned from a sharpened mussel shell with barbs on each side of the keen point, securely bound in place with braided wild cherry bark and attached to a strong line from six to twenty feet in length. The shaft, of selected yew wood, was about fifteen feet long, with one end inserted between the barbs of the harpoon blade.

When the whale was harpooned the shaft would become detached and could be hauled back to the canoe. To each line was fastened an air-filled buoy made of hair-seal hide taken off whole and dried with the hair inside. All openings were made airtight and the skin blown up like an immense balloon. The short lanyard was used when the whale was harpooned in the head and had one such buoy attached. The long line was used when the body was struck and had three buoys fastened to it. When a number of these unwieldly floats were made fast to the whale its movements were greatly impeded and it was obliged to remain on or near the surface, unable to sound deeply and perhaps drag the hunters' canoe under deep water behind it. These floats also prevented the whale from sinking after it had been killed.

The hunters were close upon their huge quarry now and Jimmy was about to see their primitive weapons in operation. The whale, a species known as a Gray, appeared to be about forty feet in length. It was still spouting intermittently and, as it swam lazily along, seemed to regard its seemingly puny assailants with indifference. But it was rudely awakened to its danger as the leading canoe darted forward and a harpoon was hurled toward it by a brawny Makah standing in the bow of the craft.

THUD! went the sharp harpoon into the broad back of the great mammal, buried almost to the shaft in the thick coat of blubber. The canoe was stopped and instantly backed; not a moment too soon, for with a sudden tremendous smash of its flukes on the water, the whale sounded, raising a great wave which nearly swamped the leading canoe and set the rest to bobbing like corks upon the troubled waters.

Each canoe, as it maneuvered into position, made fast to the craft ahead. No sooner was this accomplished than up from the depths came the monster with a fearful lurch and, as he started for the open sea, the line of canoes was towed along at a tremendous pace, Jack's little craft bringing up the rear. Its owner sat as rigid as stone watching every movement, his knife poised ready to cut the tow line in case anything happened to imperil his canoe.

As for Jimmy, with eyes and mouth wide open and the air whistling past his ears, he sat in the bottom of the canoe, gripping the thwarts tightly and taking in every phase of the thrilling chase. He had never traveled at such a rate of speed before and was far too thrilled and excited to notice that he was being soaked to the skin by the spume sent flying by the wounded whale. As the great beast yawed and turned, trying to shake off the harpoon, Jimmy was sometimes so close that he could see the individual barnacles on the leathery hide and the big blow-hole through which the spray was cascading skyward to blend with the spray of their swift passage through the water.

Four or five miles were run at this terrific speed before the pace slackened. Jimmy glanced to the left and was surprised to see the grim bulk of Cape Flattery close ahead and the open Pacific beyond. It seemed only brief moments had passed since the first harpoon had been made fast in the whale's back.

No sooner had the whale paused in its headlong rush than another canoe quickly took the lead and its harpooner sunk his weapon deep in the great back. This occasioned another wild rush, but this one was much shorter than the first. This procedure was repeated again and again, until every canoe of the flotilla had sunk its harpoon and the now exhausted monster, festooned with floats and unable to dive, gave up its efforts to escape.

At this point Jimmy found that whale hunting had its grimmer aspects. He had often seen the great animals rolling and blowing in the long swells of the Pacific and he had viewed them as impersonally as the offshore rocks and reefs. It had never occurred to him that anything so huge could awaken compassion.

But as the hunters thrust keen lances into the great body, seeking a vital spot, the whale, in its dying throes, gave cries and moans like an anguished human being. This, Jimmy realized, was no cold-blooded fish, but an animal which breathed air and felt pain and anguish much as humans do. He was deeply moved and even stolid Jack was led to admit, "Me never like to hear that sound. Too much like mother crying for its baby."

At last a merciful death thrust was given, the great animal made a last convulsive lunge in the blood-reddened water and the long battle was over.

A long and laborious tow to land now ensued and it was well on toward evening before the village was reached. Almost the entire population had assembled on the beach to await the triumphant return of the hunters and, at high tide, hundreds of willing hands dragged the prize as far as possible up the beach.

Great fires were kindled on the beach and, as the outgoing tide exposed the whale's huge proportions, knife, axe and saw were brought into play as the Indians swarmed over the carcass to quickly dismember it. The honor piece, extending entirely around the animal and including the dorsal fin, became the property of the hunter whose skilled harpoon had been the first to strike.

The chief of the tribe also claimed his share of the choicest portions, according to ancient custom. The task of stripping meat and blubber was continued through the night until there was nothing left by a few well-cleaned bones for the village dogs to fight and snarl over.

The lean part of the whale is eaten by the Indians after being boiled or baked, but the fatty portion, or blubber, is given quite an elaborate treatment, being cut into strips by the women and then boiled to extract the oil. The oil in turn is skimmed off and boiled again, after which it is placed in receptacles for food.

The blubber itself is hung up in the lodge rafters near the smoke hole and when cured looks much like fat bacon. The oil was considered a great luxury by all the Northwest tribes and constituted a popular item of barter among them.

Lighthouse Jack's conscience began to nag him before the work of butchering the whale had been completed, for he recalled that Jimmy had been entrusted to his care with the understanding that they were embarking only on a routine clam-digging expedition. Now it was dark and long past the dinner hour at the McCurdy house and the parents of his small companion were no doubt much worried.

Jimmy was reluctant to leave the beach until the final curtain was rung down on the bizarre scene, but Jack finally bribed him with whale meat and a promise to tell him a great legend of the whale god next day.

Jimmy's mother had indeed become somewhat alarmed at his long absence and was greatly relieved when he appeared, wet and breathless and proudly bearing a huge piece of whale steak.

As he recited the thrilling details of the whale hunt, his mother's first impulse was to scold Lighthouse Jack severely for taking her small son on such a hazardous venture, but as she watched the bright happiness in his eyes she decided to compromise by serving notice that Jimmy was to participate in no more whale hunts.

It is hardly necessary to add that Jimmy was looked upon as quite a hero by his comrades of the Neah Bay younger set and envied accordingly.

CHAPTER FIFTEEN

Thunderbird and Whale God

Lighthouse Jack was as good as his word, for the day after the whale hunt he appeared at the McCurdy house bearing a peace offering for Jimmy's mother in the form of a beautiful King salmon carefully wrapped in an old copy of the Washington Territory *Chronicle*. Reassured that he was to be spared the tongue-lashing he suspected he deserved, the mail carrier proposed that Jimmy accompany him on a codfishing excursion at a favorite spot of his just off Koitlah Point. He promised solemnly to stay close to shore and to return Jimmy safely well before dinner time.

Fishing for the deep-swimming rock cod was a quiet pursuit, well suited for the telling of Jack's promised whale god legend and, as the day was bright and sunny and the waters outside the bay peaceful as a pond, the expedition was duly approved. Jack's canoe was moored just off the beach, equipped with long hand lines and bits of well-seasoned clam meat for bait, and in short order the two fishermen were headed toward the blue water of the Strait.

Lighthouse Jack took the canoe in a long, lazy curve, circling well out into the Strait before heading back toward the offshore rocks of Koitlah Point.

As the canoe lifted to the gentle swell of the broad waterway Jimmy looked about him, convinced that Lighthouse Jack was right; this wild corner of the nation must be the most beautiful place in the world. The water around them was a briskly moving carpet of deep blue and sparkling white. To the left lay the distant, blue-green shore of Vancouver Island . . . the Graveyard . . . but it didn't look like a fearsome lee shore on this lovely day. Its base looked green and gentle in the distance, its gray fangs hidden in the light mist of a summer morning. Above the green of the tidal forests rose blue mountains, shining against the paler blue of the sky.

To the right, above the sombre green of the great rain forest, lay the mighty rampart of the Olympics, lifting icy, crenelated peaks thousands of feet into the soft morning sky.

As the canoe slid cleanly toward the outthrust arm of Koitlah Point, the great peaks hid themselves again behind the jagged curtain of the forest. Soon the Indian sent the canoe's stone anchor splashing overboard and handed Jimmy a length of fishline wound neatly on a carved cedar spindle. As the lines angled down into the blue-green depths of salt water, Lighthouse Jack settled himself comfortably in the stern and began to tell the legend of the whale god and Thunderbird.

Ages ago, according to Jack, Thunderbird, whose true name was *Ats-so-quat,* had his home on the rocky shore of the Pacific not far south of Cape Flattery. He was the god of the upper air and it was the beating of his enormous wings . . . a mile from tip to tip . . . that created the thunder. His eyes, resembling great diamonds, were the source of the lightning. Even when Thunderbird was not making lightning his eyes were so dazzling in their lustre that the Indians could view them only through polished horn or a piece of thin shell.

Thunderbird controlled the rain, too, so the productivity of the soil was largely dependent on him. On that account he was much courted and flattered by the Makahs and other neighboring tribes; so much so that Whale god became very jealous.

Whale god finally demanded of the Indians that they decide once and for all who was to be their chief god . . . Thunderbird or himself. The tribesmen, unwilling to incur the wrath of either powerful being, called upon wise Owl god to advise them. After much consideration, Owl god gave this decision:

"Thunderbird has served you faithfully and has never injured you and it is not in his heart to do so. But Whale god, who rules the sea, has the power to do you great harm. He can strew the sea with wrecked canoes and drown your hunters and fishermen by the scores. You have suffered through his rage many times, but nothing that has happened in the past can compare with what he might do if you offend him now. Therefore I advise that, above all, you keep peace with Whale god."

When Thunderbird learned of this he was deeply wounded in spirit and resolved to leave the ungrateful Makahs. So, accompanied by his three small Thunderbirds, he winged his way up the Strait of Juan de Fuca looking for a new home.

Rounding *Kam-Kam-ho,* the headland now called Point Wilson which marks the beginning of Puget Sound, he saw a huge rock perched on the edge of a cliff not far up the beach. Underneath was a small settlement of the Clallam tribe. This location pleased him and he and his young birds took possession of the great boulder above the village. Thunderbird was much honored by the Clallams, a fact which again aroused the jealousy of Whale god, who set his waves to eating away

110

at the beach until the bluff which supported Thunderbird's rock began to crumble.

Finally the great rock projected partly over the edge of the cliff and it was only the tremendous weight of Thunderbird that kept it from crashing down to destroy the village of the Clallams. Knowing this, the good Thunderbird refused to move from his position.

The little Thunderbirds did their best to care for the Clallams, but they were only amateurs and their efforts did not meet with the approval of the villagers. Finally the tribe took Thunderbird to task, scolding him for neglecting his tasks; rains had been lacking, the fish had remained far out at sea and everything was very bad.

Thunderbird tried to explain that only his weight was holding the dangerous boulder in place, but this contention was ridiculed by the rash young men of the tribe.

"You are not the only one who can hold that rock in place," they said. "Ten of us will take your place while you fly far up into the heavens and bring down the rain we need so sorely."

Thunderbird had grown weary of the constant complaining of the Clallams and so he finally agreed to comply with their foolhardy demands. The young Indians took up their position on the boulder, whereupon the great bird flew so high in the air that he appeared no bigger than a humming-bird and proceeded to brew a tempest such as the Clallams had never seen before.

The lightning was so glaring and incessant that the Indians were blinded and the awful crash of thunder rocked the very mountains. Lodges collapsed and such torrents of rain fell that the sea overran its shores and lost its salty taste. In an agony of fear, the Clallams begged Thunderbird to end this awful storm. Being, at heart, a gentle creature, he at length consented to do so.

In the meantime, what he had predicted transpired; no sooner had he risen into the sky than the young Indians felt a convulsive shudder animate the mighty boulder upon which they sat. Then it began to rock back and forth, slowly at first but gaining greater momentum at every movement. Realizing that their efforts to hold it in place were hopeless, the young braves leaped from their precarious position. They were barely in time, for at that instant, with an earth-shaking roar, the boulder toppled from its ancient resting place and went crashing down upon the beach village of the Clallams, leveling houses and killing many of the inhabitants. And there the giant stone lies to this very day.

With his lofty nesting place now destroyed and, disgusted with the ingratitude of the Clallams who had proven themselves as bad as the Makahs, Thunderbird summoned his three children and flew with them back down the Strait and far out over the Pacific.

Out beyond the most distant loom of land, Thunderbird looked down and saw his ancient enemy, Whale god, sporting in the waves of the ocean. Thunderbird's gentle nature had been soured by the perfidy of the tribes he had tried to serve and he flexed his great talons, eager to do battle with his old antagonist. Darting down upon Whale god, he fastened his talons in the huge form and struggled to lift it from the water. Whale god labored titanically to drag Thunderbird into the depths of the sea.

This mighty struggle brought retribution to the Makahs, for the beating of Thunderbird's wings created a terrible storm, while the struggles of Whale god set up a tidal wave, which engulfed the Makah village and killed many of the tribesmen.

The fight continued for many hours, the little Thunderbirds helping their parent as best they could. They had been growing in strength and at last, by their united efforts, they were able to lift Whale god high out of the ocean and fly with him to the topmost peak of the Olympics.

Here they devoured Whale god, leaving an immense pile of bones in a spot well known to the ancient Indians. And, in a cavern near at hand, the Thunderbirds still hold their lonely vigil. Although the Makahs have carved many images of Thunderbird and set them up to lure him back, he remembers the shabby treatment he received from them and will not return to the dwelling places of men.

This narrative of Lighthouse Jack had received many interruptions as he paused to haul big black cod or brilliantly red snapper aboard the canoe. Jimmy, too, was enjoying the best of luck. And so, by the time the tale of Thunderbird and Whale god was ended, the sun was well on its way toward the rim of the Pacific and the bottom of the canoe was piled with fish.

As the canoe drifted through the quiet waters of the bay the gentle mist that had veiled the lower reaches of Vancouver Island all day began to rise and move across the Strait. From out at sea came a short, tentative blast of the Tatoosh fog horn. Captain Samson must have sniffed the weather and ordered the boiler fired up, Jimmy thought.

It would be pleasant to sleep snug that night, lulled by the mellow cry of the distant horn and dreaming, perhaps, of mighty Thunderbird in his lonely aerie high above the sea and the forest.

CHAPTER SIXTEEN

Dark Winter

The second year of the McCurdy's stay at Neah Bay, 1878, came in on the wings of a series of crashing North Pacific storms. The shining mountains and the neighboring shore of Vancouver Island remained hidden behind black clouds which marched interminably in from the sea. Torrential rains beat down almost continuously until the little creek roared like a cataract and the village roads became dreary quagmires. It was the beginning of a year which was to bring changes and tragedy with it.

In spite of the dismal weather which kept most of the citizens of Neah Bay indoors, word spread fast through the village that Indian Agent Walton was to be replaced by Captain Charles Willoughby, a former shipmaster whose adventures had become legendary in the Pacific Northwest and who had been a neighbor of the McCurdy family in Port Townsend.

Captain Willoughby was regarded as a particular hero by Jimmy and his friends for having made several record passages in sailing vessels between San Francisco and Puget Sound. This was an era when the eyes of young America were focused on the sea and record-breaking shipmasters were regarded with the same veneration as are today's heroes of the race track and the sports arena.

The new Indian Agent had first sailed from his home town of New London as a ship's cabin boy when only twelve years old and at 21 was master of a brig sailing from the Atlantic Coast for Honolulu and Pacific Coast ports. He had come to the Puget Sound country in the early 1860's as captain of the pioneer Sound steamboat *Eliza Anderson*, later serving as sailing master of the government surveying brig *Fauntleroy*, in which service he had helped draw up the chart that Jimmy had studied in the keepers' house on Tatoosh Island.

Soon he became master and one-third owner of the bark *Narramissic*, sailing between Port Townsend and San Francisco with cargoes of lumber and piling. On a north-bound voyage in December, 1863, Captain Willoughby had on board

113

as passengers the wife of the territorial Collector of Internal Revenue P. D. Moore, her five small children and three young ladies who were to become school teachers in Washington Territory. The bark was loaded with a small consignment of general stores and carried a quantity of pig-iron in the hold for ballast.

Strong winds and heavy seas beset the *Narramissic* from the very beginning of the voyage and continued to harry her all the way up the coast. The welcome sight of Cape Flattery Light was made out after a terrible voyage of eighteen days, but it gave the ship's company only brief encouragement.

Another storm, worse than any of the others, drove the vessel far out to sea, causing her ballast to shift until she lay over at a frightening angle to the smashing seas. The gale had torn her canvas to shreds and she was completely unmanageable, but at last some whim of the changing wind and ocean currents drove her back toward the grim ships' graveyard of Vancouver Island.

To make matters worse, one of the Moore children, a little girl had become deathly ill and Captain Willoughby realized that the child was afflicted with the deadly smallpox. Although he knew there was no real cure for this terrible malady, he treated her as best he could with the limited remedies of the ship's medicine chest. She responded to this rude treatment and seemed to be recovering when the baby boy was stricken and in a short time succumbed to the disease.

The storm had, in the meantime, driven the ship into Barkley Sound, where she miraculously cleared the outlying reefs and came to anchor in sheltered waters. Here the captain fashioned a coffin for the tiny body and it was buried on desolate Diana Island.

Nor were the troubles of the unlucky *Narramissic* over. Soon a swarm of warpainted Northern savages surrounded the vessel in their canoes, demanding permission to come on board. Captain Willoughby ordered his crew to hoist the heavy pig-iron billets from the ship's hold and line the rails with them, ready to hurl into the canoes should any attempt be made to board the ship by force.

The captain finally allowed the chief and a few of his followers to come aboard. Roaming about the decks, the chief caught sight of the women and children in a frightened group on the quarterdeck. He beckoned them imperiously to come nearer, but Captain Willoughby held up a warning hand and pronounced the dread word—*"smallpox!"*

Forgetting his dignity, the chief gave a startled gasp and dove headlong over the rail, his braves following him in a frenzy of fear. The canoes paused only long enough to pull the chief and his followers aboard and then were in full flight toward the bay's entrance.

114

The single word, *smallpox,* was more feared by the Indians than loaded cannon, for they had felt its deadly ravages. Several years before, a raiding party of Northern Indians had crossed the Strait and stolen a quantity of clothing and blankets from a "pest house," or smallpox hospital, on the American side. These infected articles were bartered far and wide, causing a smallpox epidemic that swept the Northwest coast, bringing death to hundreds of Indians.

The *Narramissic* finally put to sea again with improvised sails of blankets and sacking. In the Strait a passing schooner provided some emergency provisions and, after a passage of more than two months, the bark reached Port Townsend, where the passengers were cared for and sent on to their destination, the territorial capital at Olympia.

Jimmy hoped the retired mariner would prove to be as willing a spinner of yarns as his friend Captain Samson, for the winter downpour made him a virtual prisoner inside four walls and the tales of such an adventurous captain would provide a welcome break in the monotony.

Even the Indians conceded that this was one of the worst winters they could remember. Storm succeeded storm, each seemingly more furious than the last. Giant billows, bred in the far reaches of the ocean and forced into the mouth of the Strait by the propelling gales, came thundering into the bay through the passage between Koitlah Point and Waadah Island.

Sweeping majestically onward, compressed and heightened by the restricting shoreline, the great waves crashed upon the beach with a force that seemed to jar the very hills behind the village. Acres of kelp, torn from its rocky fastenings, was cast upon the shore in great interwoven heaps.

There were no "good spells" in that winter's weather, but during brief lulls in the worst of it, the village boys including Jimmy and his brothers, used their best powers of persuasion to gain permission for outdoor excursions. Their parents, whose resistance was worn down by months of close association with their restless children, became more lenient as the dreary winter progressed. On such occasions Jimmy found the wave-battered village beach an exciting place. Dressed in miniature sailor's oilskin slicker and sou'-wester and wearing a pair of red-topped black boots which had been given him at Christmas by one of the pilots from the pilot-schooner *Indra,* he joined his friends in mock battles against the giant kelp.

Imagining that they were attacking a multitude of sleeping savages, the boys swung improvised war-clubs to crack open the large citron-colored kelp heads. Added grim satisfaction was given the one-sided mock battles by the fact that when the giant bulbs were broken by a smash blow they emitted a hollow, groaning sound. Sometimes they tried to disentangle the slippery stems attached to the bulbs, each seeking to find the longest piece of the sinuous, whiplike growth. Sections forty or fifty feet long and almost as strong and pliable as ship's hawsers were not unusual.

Ships passing through the Strait during this vicious winter were often subjected to the full force of a sudden storm and many of the lumber schooners lost their deckloads. Even coasting steamers, in several instances, had to jettison cargo in order to withstand the battering of the sea.

During one brief lull in the series of storms the beach was covered with milled lumber washed from the deck of some hard-pressed schooner. This had hardly been salvaged by the Indians when a miscellaneous cargo came floating into the bay. There were sacks of flour, boxes of apples, kegs of butter, crates of vegetables and other foodstuffs. The Makahs eagerly launched their canoes despite the heavy surf to return loaded with jetsam which told as plainly as words that some vessel was battling to keep afloat somewhere off Cape Flattery. The salvaged flour was caked for an inch or so around the outside of the sacks, but was otherwise none the worse for its immersion. Although a salty tang had been added to the fruit and vegetables, they were still edible.

Jimmy and his companions, unable to take to the water, patrolled the shoreline, beachcombing for items overlooked by the Indians. They secured a little of everything that came ashore and piled their plunder safely out of reach of the waves. Wet and shivering, they were about to carry their hard-won treasure home when a passing Indian, viewing the spoils with a calculating eye, roughly ordered them off and confiscated the entire store.

Their indignation knew no bounds and they loudly disputed with the plunderer, but to no avail. The surly Indian told them that everything that came ashore on a reservation belonged to the Makahs. He then ordered them to *"Hyak klatawah"* . . . go away in a hurry, backing up his command with a wicked flourish of the fish-skinning knife which he whipped out of his belt.

The boys wisely abandoned their salvaged goods and proceeded, with empty hands and bitter hearts, to carry their tale of woe to that unofficial arbiter of village disputes, Captain Zem.

"I'm sorry, boys," the old trader told them, "but there's nothing you can do about it. You see, an Injun's a king on his own reservation and can get away with about anything he pleases short of murder. It was less than two years ago that Colonel Custer and the whole Seventh Cavalry was wiped out back on the plains. The Makahs aren't as savage as the Sioux, maybe, but they ain't as civilized as you might think either."

Captain Zem's deep blue eyes usually twinkled when he talked to his young friends, but he looked serious as he continued, "I've got a government trader's license and I been here

116

since before your ma's and pa's was born, but these natives could put me out of business in a hurry if they decided to. It's the same with all the white folks working here, so we just have to take our medicine and like it if we want to stay here."

With this poor consolation the boys had to be content, but Jimmy never again felt quite the same toward the Makahs who had seemed so friendly and easy-going during the pleasant days of summer. And thereafter when he or his friends found anything of value on the beach they took great care to keep it hidden from the sight of any prying Indian.

When the tide was high the boys found that the crashing surf cut deeply into the beach, sometimes uncovering objects that had long been hidden from human eyes. While combing the beach one day they were surprised to find a massive section of ship's keel imbedded in the sand. Attached to the keel were oaken ribs, splintered and charred by fire.

The boys reported their find to the trader who, as usual, was able to shed enlightenment on the mystery.

"So that old wreck has showed up again," he mused. "It's the remains of the American ship *Ellen Foster*, Captain Anderson, from Callao for Puget Sound, that went ashore in the winter of '67. She made her landfall off Flattery on a December morning, but a strong easterly kept her from makin' any headway until the next morning, when she caught a light nor'easter that put her well up the Strait. But a hurricane came tearin' in from the southeast and she ran for Neah Bay. She made it inside, but both anchors wouldn't hold her and she dragged on the reef. The crew made it ashore in the lifeboat, but somehow the wreck caught on fire and burned to the water's edge. The sand gradually covered up what was left of her, but every five years or so the waves bring it up again. I remember how disappointed the Injuns were when the fire robbed them of the loot they'd been countin' on."

It seemed almost as if the resurrection of the long-buried *Ellen Foster* was an omen of things to come, for in a few days a howling westerly came raging in to send ocean combers high on the beach at Neah Bay. Then, like a great wind-driven bird, a square-rigged ship came scudding into the bay under closely reefed sails. As she swung under the lee of Waadah Island her anchor was let go with a rush, but even in this partial protection she rolled and pitched sickeningly, for she was in ballast and rising high to wind and waves. It was soon evident to those on shore that the tall sailing ship was being gradually driven closer to the beach.

"She's dragging anchor," exclaimed Captain Zem, who had joined the awe-struck group of villagers on the beach in front of his store. "She's in poor holding ground and if they don't watch out they'll pile up for sure."

By this time the crew of the square-rigger had realized

117

their peril and a second anchor was dropped, but the big vessel continued to roll and pitch so dreadfully that it seemed the anchors might be torn loose at any moment.

The ship was a three-master, her long gray hull striped with painted white ports and showing red below the water line. A storm-shredded red British merchant ensign whipped from her mizzen gaff and Captain Zem pronounced her "a typical English lime-juicer."

For two days the ship clung to her anchors in the raging sea, at one moment almost rolling her yard-arms under; the next rising on a giant wave to expose a long expanse of red bilge. It was obviously impossible for the crew to launch a boat or, if they could, to land one through the terrible surf that lashed the bay.

The Makahs kept a death-watch on the beach, their greedy eyes fixed hopefully on the imperilled ship. Probably not one among them but hoped that she would be driven ashore, for she would provide rich pickings to these veteran looters of wrecked ships. As for Jimmy and his friends, they were in almost as great a fever of excitement as were the Indians. They told each other that they hoped the beautiful big ship escaped, but if she *did* go ashore they hoped it would be in the daytime so they could view the thrilling sight.

But by some miracle the anchors held and, on the third day, the storm subsided. The ship's crew, haggard and half famished, landed upon the beach in a ship's boat and were provided with hot food and coffee by the white citizens of Neah Bay. They explained that for a week they had been subsisting on hardtack and cold water, for the cook had been unable to keep a fire in the galley range and most of their stores had been consumed on the long voyage from Australia. Their ship was the *Iona,* bound for Puget Sound and a cargo of lumber.

Late that afternoon the mill tug *Richard Holyoke* came steaming into the bay, the *Iona's* trusty anchors came clanking up and she was drawn smoothly toward the open Strait.

Jimmy felt like cheering, but when he saw the glum faces of the disappointed Indians who surrounded him on the beach, he decided he had better not.

CHAPTER SEVENTEEN

Farewell to Neah Bay

As Jimmy listened to the storm winds rattle the very boards of the sturdy house at night, and the unceasing rain pound like fists upon the cedar-shingled roof, he often thought of the pilot schooner *Indra,* stationed off the grim Cape in the path of Straits-bound ships. The *Indra* was a staunch 75-foot craft, trim and handy as a yacht. She was commanded by Captain Henry Winslow, a veteran of a lifetime aboard the coasting schooners of the Pacific.

The pilot schooner was expected to remain on station regardless of the weather, for at any moment there might come a signal for a pilot to guide an incoming ship up the Strait of Juan de Fuca and through the tortuous channels of Puget Sound to her loading port. The little ship was a frequent visitor at Neah Bay, where her crew put in for mail and supplies. The *Indra,* with her glistening white hull, graceful lines and two gallantly raked masts, was the prettiest ship ever built. Besides, stationed on the schooner was Pilot Peter Cutler, who was a frequent visitor at the McCurdy house. Jimmy, whose soaring spirit of adventure could not be thwarted by his lameness, was a great favorite of the big seaman, who brought him frequent gifts, including the beautiful red-topped boots which were his pride and joy.

It seemed to Jimmy a rather hard fate that doomed the *Indra* and Peter Cutler to a perpetual vigil off the stormy Cape, but he knew that great ships might be lost if the little pilot schooner were missing in an hour of need. He was sure, too, that his friend, the pilot, would not be happy in a safe shoreside job, but on stormy nights he couldn't help thinking of the little craft fighting the great, sweeping waves of the open ocean and wishing she were snugged down in a safe anchorage.

Late January and early February brought swirling snow gusts from the north to vary the monotony of unending rain. Waadah Island and other distant points appeared only occasionally through the driving scud, their bold outlines softened by a light blanket of snow. The boys were hopeful that the snow would soon be deep enough for coasting on the steep hills back of the village.

During this squally weather Jimmy happened, one afternoon, to glance out over the bay. Through a rift in the storm clouds he caught a glimpse of a small schooner, close-hauled and heeling over as she rounded Koitlah Point. She resembled a ghost ship, with white hull and sails framed for a brief instant in a patch of wintry sky. Although the picture was obscured in a moment, Jimmy's sharp eyes had recognized the incoming ship as his beloved *Indra.*

Soon she came slowly through the enveloping mists to an anchorage in the bay. Jimmy felt a brief thrill of delight at the prospect of a visit from his favorite ship and his friend, but his joy turned quickly to dismay as the *Indra* swung 'round on her anchor to display her flag drooping sadly at half-mast.

Running as fast as he could at his queer, lopsided gait, he burst into his father's shop. "Oh, Dad," he announced in an awed and breathless voice, "the *Indra's* just come in and her flag's half-masted!"

His father moved to the window for a searching look at the anchored pilot boat. "You're right, Jimmy," he said gravely, "It's the *Indra,* sure enough, and she's flying a distress signal. I wonder what's happened."

As soon as the schooner was anchored a boat was dropped and was now being rowed ashore by a single person. As Jimmy and his father hurried to the beach they saw that the solitary oarsman was Captain Winslow, the *Indra's* skipper. As the boat's prow grounded on the beach the captain clambered stiffly out to walk slowly toward them, his head bowed.

"Who was it?" Mr. McCurdy asked as he met the captain and laid his hand upon the old seaman's bent shoulder. A half-masted ensign could mean only one thing, he knew; death had brushed the *Indra* with wings darker than the storm's.

"Peter Cutler . . . the best friend I ever had," the captain answered in a choked voice.

Jimmy, fighting back the tears that almost blinded him, followed the two men up the path to the McCurdy house. Inside the small living room, Captain Winslow silently took a dark object from beneath his heavy seacoat. He smoothed it slowly into shape and reverently laid it upon the table.

"Peter's sou'wester," he said simply. "We found it floating in the water."

Mr. McCurdy guided the captain gently to a chair beside the stove and Jimmy's mother came quietly from the kitchen with a mug of steaming coffee in her hand. Striving to control his emotions, the *Indra's* master went on:

"We were about ten miles off the Cape trying to find the English bark *Dartmoor Castle* when a blinding snow squall hit us. The flakes were big as feathers and they froze on everything

120

as fast as they fell. The deck was like glass from the snow and frozen spray and we couldn't see a boat's length ahead. Then suddenly the wind veered and hit us from another quarter. The *Indra* heeled over and the main boom swept across the deck. It caught Peter a terrible blow on the side of the head and knocked him right over the rail into the sea.

He was weighted down with his heavy sea-coat and rubber boots and he never had a chance . . . even if the blow hadn't knocked him unconscious. We threw life preservers overside and brought the schooner about as fast as we could, but all we ever found was his sou'wester floating near the life preservers."

During this recital Jimmy sat weeping silently in a corner, hardly able to believe that he would never see his big, weather-beaten friend again. He knew that he could never again put to sea with Lighthouse Jack without the terrible vision of his friend Peter Cutler struggling for his life in the seething waves ten miles off shore while the *Indra* circled about in the darkness making her hopeless attempt at rescue . . . and in the center of that circle the tiny black dot of a sou'wester.

But Jimmy's days at Neah Bay were numbered and he was destined to make no more summer voyages in Jack's canoe. Ever since his mother had been hurled into the surf by the overturning of the boat which first brought them to the village she had been troubled by a painful cough which grew progressively worse. This winter of fog, rain and cold winds from the nearby ocean had worsened her condition and Doctor Howell, deeply concerned, advised her husband to take her to a healthier climate as soon as possible.

The mother only laughed at their fears, insisting that she was as well off at Neah Bay as anywhere; that there was nothing seriously wrong with her and, furthermore, that she didn't intend to abandon her family to the care of an Indian house-keeper . . . not even one as well-meaning as Quedessa.

The Indians, however, by some strange instinct, seemed to sense that all was not well at the McCurdy house. Suddenly they refused to sell fish to Jimmy's father, a puzzling development since normally they were more than eager to convert part of their abundant catch to white men's money.

For a while Captain Zem's trading post supplied seafood to the McCurdy table, but one day the old storekeeper announced, "I'm mighty sorry, Mac, but the Indians have served notice on me I'm not to sell you any more fish."

"Why not?" his customer asked angerly.

Captain Zem looked embarrassed. "Haven't you heard of their belief that if a fish is sold to a family where there's bad sickness all the rest of the fish will get mad and leave these waters?"

Jimmy's father looked as if he were convinced the old trader and the Indians had all taken leave of their senses.

"I know it's a crazy idea," the trader admitted, spreading his hands helplessly, "but it's no use tryin' to argefy 'em out of it and they'll stop sellin' to me if I sell to you. They'll be watchin' me pretty close, but I'll manage to see that you get a fish now and then. I'll put it in a flour sack and stuff paper around it so it'll look like a sack of flour. You can come down after dark and carry it home, but we can't work that scheme too often. If them Injuns catch me at it there'll be an awful ruckus."

When Lighthouse Jack heard that his friends had been deprived of this staple of Neah Bay diet he turned the finest specimens of his daily catch over to Quedessa. At great risk to herself and her husband, the faithful Indian woman smuggled the forbidden food to the McCurdy house at night, the fish carefully concealed under her blanket. When Jimmy's mother told her gently that she must not take this risk Quedessa begged, with tears running down her seamed face, to be allowed to show her gratitude in this poor way to the one who had brought her little boy back from the shadowy land of death.

Quedessa's willing sacrifice was not to continue for long, however. Mrs. McCurdy could no longer conceal the pain that made each breath a torment. Finally she gave up the struggle and agreed to be taken to her sister's comfortable home in Portland, the largest city in the Pacific Northwest. It was arranged that Mr. McCurdy should accompany his wife as far as Tacoma, where she and Jimmy would travel by the newly built Northern Pacific Railroad to Portland. Bill and Frank were left in the care of the new Indian Agent's family.

As the steamboat moved slowly out of the bay, Jimmy saw the familiar canoe of Lighthouse Jack anchored off the Koitlah Point rocks. He knew the steamer would swing close to the codfishing rocks when it rounded the point and he hurried to the starboard rail.

The smell of coming spring was in the air and the distant bulk of Vancouver Island loomed on the horizon ahead. Far out on the waters of Juan de Fuca's Strait a tall bark moved gracefully toward the Cape and the open Pacific, drawn by the invisible hawser of a tugboat that fussed along under a ragged banner of black smoke. An Indian canoe slashed past the steamer, its floorboards heaped with shining fish, a flotilla of gliding seagulls crying in its wake.

Then the steamer was sweeping past Koitlah Point, picking up speed. The thrust of its bow wave set the canoe of Lighthouse Jack to bobbing lightly and he looked up, surprised, in the preoccupation of his fishing, to see the moving bulk so close beside him.

Jimmy leaned far over the rail, waving wildly to this good friend. "Goodbye!" he cried shrilly. "Goodbye, Lighthouse Jack!

I'll come back when mamma's feeling better . . . so don't catch all the fish!"

The steamer was drawing away fast from the land now and Jimmy had to face clear aft to see Lighthouse Jack. The Makah was standing easily in his rocking canoe, one hand raised in farewell, and the sound of his voice was small and far away.

"*Klahowya!*" he shouted. "*Klahowya,* Tenas Yaw-ka-duke![12] I will save space in the canoe for you!"

Klahowya is a word that means both goodbye and hello, but the *Tamahnous* of Lighthouse Jack . . . the spirit that lives with an Indian and sometimes counsels him . . . told him that his small friend's gentle mother was embarked on the long journey from which there is no return.

But he knew, too, that the spell of this mystic place of sea and forest and great mountains was very strong. Someday, he was sure, his white friend would return to visit Neah Bay.

In the meantime, he would be careful that he did not catch all the fish.

* * * * END * * * *

---

[12] In his book *By Juan de Fuca's Strait*, Mr. McCurdy wrote, "While living on the reservation I won the friendship of an old Indian fisherman. When he returned from the fishing ground I was usually on hand to greet him and help him pull his little canoe up on the beach. If the day had been successful I was given a fish to take home. The Indians seemed much amused by this friendship and they began to call me 'Tenas (little) Yaw-ka-duke', while my friend was laughingly addressed as 'Hyas (big) Yaw-ka-duke'. Our close association lasted as long as I remained on the reservation.

While visiting the reservation years later one of the older Indians with a smile greeted me by my old name of Yaw-ka-duke. My curiosity was awakened and I asked the meaning of the mysterious word which had been applied to me when a small boy upon the Neah Bay beach, and to my old friend as well.

"Why, that means 'partner' in the Makah language. The Indians used to say that you and the old man were partners in the fishing business. Your old partner never forgot you and often asked about 'Tenas Ya-ka-duke' ", was the reply."